MEMENTO MORI

MEMENTO MORI

The Gravestones
of
Early Long Island

1680—1810

Richard F. Welch

Friends for Long Island's Heritage
Syosset, New York

Library of Congress Cataloging in Publication Data

Welch, Richard F.
Memento Mori: the gravestones of early Long Island, 1680–1810.

  Bibliography: p.
  Includes index.
1. Sepulchral monuments—New York (State)—Long
Island.
2. Sepulchral monuments—New England. I. Title
NB1856.L66W44   1983   736'.5'0974   83–9027
ISBN 0–911357–00–9
ISBN 0–911357–01–7 (pbk.)

Table of Contents

Foreword

The Friends for Long Island's Heritage are pleased to present Richard Welch's scholarly study of Long Island gravestones as the initiation of an expanded publication program to record and interpret our area's natural and historic heritage. Mr. Welch has traveled the length and breadth of the Island and comprehensively researched the original historical sources relating to gravestones and their carvers.

Gravestones constitute a significant body of colonial period artifacts still extant and provide cultural and artistic insights of early American life. Mr. Welch's study illuminates the rich resource that exists on Long Island and sets forth an invaluable permanent guide to the early gravestones, markers, and historic cemeteries in our small villages. We hope that this study will create greater awareness among the public, local officials, and family cemetery guardians, and stimulate greater efforts and resources to preserve these valuable folk art memorials of our colonial heritage.

Norman Tengstron
President, Friends for Long Island's Heritage

Acknowledgements

A book covering such a multi-faceted topic as early Long Island gravestones and their carvers could not have been written without the help of many generous people. The staffs at the New-York Historical Society, the Historical Documents Collection, Queens College, and the East Hampton Free Library provided valuable assistance in tracing probate records and accounts of gravestone carvers. Similar service was rendered by the staff at the Long Island Room of the Queensborough Public Library, Jamaica. Many people aided me in tracing or gaining admittance to private burial grounds. I would like to thank William Strong, Norman O'Berry, and Mrs. Garry Ketcham especially.

I also wish to extend my gratitude to Ronald Manfredi for his photographic assistance. I am obligated to James Slater and Ralph Tucker for helping sort out the careers of the Manning and Lamson families on Long Island. A special debt is owed Anthony Miracolo, Jr., Robert Mackay, Francis Duval, and Ivan Rigby who provided useful criticism. Needless to say, none of the persons mentioned above bears responsibility for flaws that may remain. Special gratitude to Edward Smits without whose foresight, enthusiasm, and perseverance, this book would not have reached completion.

My wife Beverly's enthusiasm, criticisms, and patience were of inestimable value. To her, I owe the greatest debt.

CHAPTER I

The Origin of the American
Gravestone-cutting Tradition, 1660–1810

American gravestone carving of the 1660–1810 period was the culmination of a funerary art tradition originating in antiquity. It was, however, the medieval interpretation of these ancient symbols of mortality and resurrection which most directly influenced the imagery carved on early American gravestones. The theocentric or ecclesiocentric nature of the Middle Ages dictated the predominance of religious themes in art. Few religious themes so attracted the artist as the mysterious moment of death and the shrouded existence of the soul in an eternity of bliss or damnation. Medieval artists had inherited from the ancient world a number of near-universal symbols of death and resurrection. These they developed to suit the strictures of Christian theology and regional, cultural, or personal taste. Mortality symbols such as skeletons and death's heads achieved widespread currency in painting and illuminated manuscript design, and in stone, wood, and metal sculpture. Medieval depictions of heavenly beings as anthropomorphical creatures eventually became the patterns for the soul effigy gravestones of the seventeenth and eighteenth centuries.

The great popularity of death and the afterlife as graphic subjects was due not only to the influence of Christian beliefs but to the precarious nature of human existence as well. High infant mortality, primitive medical knowledge, and cyclical famines and wars all served to make death an ever-visible presence in medieval life. In the fourteenth century, a new and particularly virulent plague appeared. The Black Death is estimated to have killed between one-third and one-half of the population of Europe, leaving in its wake not only a decimated population but important political and social changes as well. In art, the effect of the plague was an increased fascination with the subject of death. Strikingly morbid protrayals of the physical corruption death leaves in its wake became popular. The "Dance of Death," a series of illustrations and woodcuts depicting death carrying away members of all classes, enjoyed wide distribution and popularity.

This obsession with the more revolting aspects of death abated as the plague receded. However, the conventional medieval funerary symbols survived intact. Skulls with and without crossbones, skeletons, winding sheets, coffins, picks and shovels, and hourglasses all passed into the folk idioms of funerary art. The religious upheavals of the Protestant Reformation did not diminish their popularity. Medieval funerary iconography was featured on printed funeral broadsides and eulogies well into the eighteenth century. The skulls, crossbones, and hourglasses used to border death and disaster notices in colonial newspapers, as well as the coffins featured on Paul Revere's print, "5 Coffings for Boston Massacre," were linear descendants of medieval progenitors. In all probability, the earliest American gravestone cutters used printed examples of funerary symbols as their first models.

The derivation of American gravestone art from medieval, particularly English medieval, antecedents does not fully explain how the traditional mortality and salvation symbols made their way from parchment, paper, and wood to stone. Nor does the medieval derivation of American gravestones fully explain why these symbols burst forth in a spectacular

Opposite: The beautifully situated Smith-Strong burial grounds overlook Setauket harbor on Long Island.

I

Modern reconstructions of seventeenth-century wooden fence-post grave markers were made for the 1978 public television production of Nathaniel Hawthorne's The Scarlet Letter.

display of design, variety, and number in the English North American colonies during the seventeenth and eighteenth centuries.

At the time of the first large-scale English migrations to the New World (1620–1660), there was no widespread method of identifying graves in England by means of stone markers.[2] During this period, English graves, with the exception of those of the nobility and gentry, were identified by wood markers constructed like a section of fence with two posts anchored in the ground and a plank fitted between them. The inscription and possibly some funerary ornament were painted on the crosspiece (illustrated). The use of similar markers on Long Island in the early years of settlement is recounted in Benjamin Thompson's description of burial practices in East Hampton: "The first interments were made in the south burial ground, and here may yet [1843] be seen monuments of red cedar probably as ancient as any now remaining."[3] Among those recorded as having had such a marker was Lion Gardiner, eponymous colonizer of Gardiner's Island, dominant force in early East Hampton history, and progenitor of the influential Gardiner family. The cedar-post memorial marking his death in 1663 was uprooted to make way for the pretentious "Gothick" monstrosity a descendant erected in 1886.[4] Time and weather have destroyed the other wood markers mentioned by Thompson. None seem to have survived on Long Island and very few anywhere in the United States.

A vernacular tradition of stonecutting was definitely established in England during the 1680s. It was stylistically distinct from American models. By this time, however, the American tradition had been established, perhaps, for as long as a generation.[5]

One of the paradoxes of the American gravestone-cutting tradition is its Puritan origins. The Puritans, as the Calvinist sects of England came to be called, originally exhibited a marked iconoclastic streak springing from their belief that the first commandment contained a prohibition against the use of religious art or symbols on any type of religious structures, including gravestones and tombs. Indeed, between 1540 and 1640 there was a great wave of destruction of English tombs and funerary monuments. Some of the destruction was caused by governmental and private looting, but much of the mutilation was meted out by members of religious sects who found religious symbols to be idolatrous.

The two greatest outbreaks of funerary monument destruction came during the reign of Edward VI and during the English civil war of the 1640s. The funerary art in monasteries, chanceries, and other religious institutions was so badly decimated in early Tudor times that Elizabeth I issued two edicts prohibiting further destruction and ordering the repair of damaged pieces.[6] During the civil war, the many memorial brasses in the great cathedrals were lost.

In developing an elaborate gravestone iconography, the American Puritans broke with their English cousins who, with one exception, never developed a similar system of rituals and art.[7] Some have attributed the appearance of carved gravestones among the American Puritans to a cultural need which overpowered religious proscriptions. Others have seen in the stones a manifestation of a human need, one which was allowed to flourish in an officially hostile society by means of a legalistic dodge which placed burial grounds under civil authority. Hence stones carved with funerary symbols were not in violation of religious law. In a more recent study, David E. Stannard has argued that the appearance of such gravestones only after 1660, and the passing of the first generation of Puritan settlers, reflects the growing sense of isolation felt by the New England Puritans.[8] This Puritan "tribalism," in which they saw themselves as the remnant of the only true band of Christ's followers on earth, magnified the death of each individual Puritan into a calamity which weakened all Puritan society. It was this sense of communal loss which resulted in elaborate burial rituals and in the use of gravestones with symbols.

American gravestone cutters freely interpreted both mortality and salvation images to suit the needs of their own churches, communities, and imaginations, as well as the size of their customers' purses. Largely without formal training, the carvers fashioned their memorials with a simplicity and naiveté which conferred a primitive power on their images. European influences ultimately overwhelmed and destroyed the native vision. But before this occurred there was to be 150 years of the flowering of one of the finest and most visible of American folk arts.

The New England Nexus

Like so much that was important in early Long Island history, early American gravestones came at first exclusively from New England. It was in New England that the American gravestone-cutting tradition first developed, and it was there that it achieved its greatest popularity and fullest development. Stones from New England were exported to Long Island, New York City, New Jersey, as far south as South Carolina and Georgia, and as far north as Nova Scotia.

Gravestones and their symbols were meant to serve a religious function and provide a lesson in theology. The great majority of the early inhabitants of New England and eastern Long Island were Puritans. Calvinism stressed the awful power of God and the helplessness of man who had been predestined before all time to an eternity of salvation or damnation. The doctrine of predestination, coupled with an emphasis on the transitory nature of earthly existence, dictated the emphasis Calvinism placed on the moment of death. Only then would the individual Puritan receive the immutable judgment of God concerning the fate of his soul in the afterlife. Underscoring the Puritan's obsession with these doctrines, the two most widespread gravestone images were the winged death's head, symbol of mortality, and the winged soul effigy, symbol of resurrection. Stones cut with these images appeared first in the Massachusetts Bay Colony around 1660; they reached Long Island about 1685.

The earliest white inhabitants of Suffolk County and most of present-day Nassau (formed from the eastern towns of Queens County when western Queens joined New York City in 1898) came from New England, and they and their descendants maintained close ties with New England for many years. Between 1640 when the first English towns on Long Island were founded and 1664 when Dutch rule in New Netherlands came to an end, those parts of Long Island not subjected to Dutch rule were under Connecticut jurisdiction.

The incorporation of all of the island under New York administration after 1664 was not popular with the transplanted New Englanders of Suffolk County. The old habit of looking across Long Island and Block Island Sounds for trade, marriage, and religious and cultural leadership died hard. Indeed, in several instances New York officials complained of the Long

Islanders' preference for trading with New England rather than the rest of New York. In 1703, Lord Cornbury, governor of New York, wrote the Lords of Trade that the people of the East End chose "to trade with the People of Boston, Connecticut, Rhode Island rather than with the People of New York."[9] Again in that same year the governor complained that the people of Suffolk were "not very willing to be persuaded to believe that they belonged to this province. They are full of New England principles."[10] In this the governor echoed the lament of Lord Bellomont in 1687 who wrote to the government in London that, "... What is produced from their [the East Ender's] industry is frequently carried to Boston ... not withstanding the many strict rules and laws made to confine them to this place."[11] This strong link between the people of the East End and New England lasted well into the eighteenth century. In 1798, John Lion Gardiner of Gardiner's Island and East Hampton recalled that, "till within thirty years Boston was the place of market for this part of Long Island."[12] Not surprisingly, then, the East Enders also brought over New England gravestones. In fact, they continued to import gravestones from New England until the art died out in the first years of the nineteenth century.

Although the New England gravestones were crafted under the influence of the area's Puritanism, they were descended from a widely shared European tradition of funerary art and hence were readily understood and appreciated by the inhabitants of the religiously heterogeneous western section of Long Island, as well as Manhattan and the mainland. The people in the latter areas first imported New England gravestones and then, in the third decade of the eighteenth century, shifted their allegiances to local stonecutters in New York City and its environs who had begun to carve similar stones in their own styles.

Death in Colonial America

In contrast to contemporary Americans, colonial Long Islanders faced death squarely and openly. There was no evasion, no euphemisms—just plain talk and lectures from the pulpit on the certain fate of mortal men. These verbal pronouncements were augmented by the symbols and epitaphs carved on gravestones.

Among the Puritans, death was not only a fact of life, it was the *central* fact of life. According to Puritan teachings, all man's earthly existence was directed towards the moment when he or she would face the Almighty in a terrible moment of truth. Since most Puritans came to be confident of their own righteousness, they could be expected to look forward to death as a time of reward for their earthly labors even if they were reluctant to leave this vale of tears any sooner than necessary.

In addition to theological doctrine, there were other reasons why death played so prominent a part in the social and religious life of the colonial Long Islander. One of the most important reasons was that death was a more frequent and visible event then. At a time when inhabitants lived in close communion with one another, social bonds were tighter and the death of one individual had a great effect on the whole community. Cemeteries were not located away from the populated areas, as is the custom today, but were centrally located, with the exception of family plots on farms.*

The people, of course, had much more frequent recourse to the burying grounds since mortality rates at that time were high. Any trip to an early

American burying ground demonstrates the high degree of infant mortality. Cotton Mather, the famous Puritan divine, fathered fourteen children of whom seven died in childhood; five of the six who reached adulthood failed to reach the age of thirty. Andrew Eliot of Boston's North Church saved the gloves which were sent as invitations to funerals. In thirty-two years he collected 3,000 pairs.[13]

Because of the religious emphasis on death, the strong communal ties, and perhaps the tedium of life, funerals developed their own somberly festive rituals. Ministers wrote both eulogies and funeral sermons which were sometimes printed as broadsides. A Long Island example of this genre is the sermon written by the Rev. Ebenezer Prime of Huntington delivered at the grave of Freelove Wilmot in 1744. The printed version of this sermon runs fifty-one pages. It is disappointing that the only funerary motif on this pamphlet is the black border on the title page.[14] As previously mentioned, gloves were sent as invitations to funerals. In addition, funeral rings, embossed with mortality symbols and the name of the deceased, were often given to friends of the family. The hearse itself was usually decorated with somber bunting on which was painted or drawn death's heads, coffins, picks and shovels, and other suitable images. The wealthy might add hatchments. The horses that pulled the hearse were often blanketed in similar mourning decorations. Funerals, like some modern religious observances, often became opportunities for ostentatious display of wealth and social standing. The problem was apparently most acute in Boston, or at least the authorities there were particularly sensitive to it, because twice in 1720–1722 and again in 1741–1742 elaborate funerals were banned.

Provincial though it was, Long Island was not without its elaborate funerals. Gabriel Furman in *Antiquities of Long Island* explains that in the eighteenth century funerals were very expensive and "it was a custom in the old families to lay up a stock of superior wine to be used on such occasions; and frequently at those funerals you would meet with wine so choice and excellent that it could scarcely be equalled by any in the land. . . ."[15]

The New England custom of giving gifts to mourners was also followed. Furman goes on to say that

> . . . when the estate of the deceased would afford it and even in many cases when it could not it was the custom to give to each of the pallbearers, clergymen, and physicians attending a scarf of white linen (sufficient in quantity to make a shirt), which was worn by them across the shoulder; and also a pair of gloves, either of silk or kid. If the deceased were old or married, the scarf was fastened with a white ribbon and the gloves were white. . . . At a still earlier period it was the custom, at the more superior order of funerals, to give gold mourning rings to each person who attended . . .[16]

*Minor variations existed between the different denominations in the location of their burial grounds. Calvinist congregations insisted that cemeteries were under civil, not ecclesiastical, administration. Hence, Congregational and Presbyterian burial grounds could be located on public land in any convenient spot in the village. On the other hand, Anglican and Dutch Reformed burial grounds were ordinarily incorporated into the churchyard itself. The placement of family burial grounds depended largely on the preferences of the families involved (illus. p. 6).

*Village cemeteries in colonial
America were usually centrally
located; one of the most picturesque
village cemeteries is the South End
burial ground, East Hampton.*

*The burial ground at the Dutch Re-
formed Church in Flatbush is incorporated into the churchyard.*

The Long Island funeral could turn into a somewhat less than dignified ritual as described in the following passage:

And even within the present century [nineteenth] it was likewise the custom at funerals in the country parts of Long Island, for the relatives of the deceased, at the house from which the funeral was to proceed, to prepare a large quantity of cold provisions, such as roast turkeys, boiled hams, roast beef etc. which were set upon a table in a room opened for the purpose, and everyone went there and helped himself as he pleased. Also rum, brandy, gin, with pipes, tabacco, and segars, were handed around among the people during their stay at the house, it being considered inhospitable not to do so; and it was not an unusual thing to see the farmers congregate together, in warm weather, under the shade of trees, about the vicinity of the house, smoking their long pipes and drinking, hearing and telling the news, and laughing and talking together for two or three hours before the funeral would move. This long stay at the house previous to proceeding to the place of inter-ment, together with the great plenty of spiritous liquors distributed about, sometimes occasioned scenes of much noise and very inap-propriate for the purpose for which they had assembled.[17]

The Dutch settlers in Brooklyn had similar funeral practices as evidenced by an itemized bill for the funeral of the mother of Wilhelmus Stoothoff written in the Dutch language and dated 1735. Funeral expenses included beer, wine, ten pair of gloves, one gross of pipes, handkerchiefs, glasses, sugar, rum, ferry money, casket, and digging the grave. Strangely, there is no mention of a gravestone. The total cost of the funeral was £9.16.3.[18]

The decline of this party-like atmosphere at wakes was credited to the Rev. Evan M. Johnson, rector of the Episcopal Church at Newtown, who, in the first half of the nineteenth century, proposed that funerals should commence within one hour of the gathering of the mourners and that spirits be dispensed with. To make this major modification acceptable to his parishioners he agreed to relinquish his claim to a funeral scarf. This plan spread from his parish to many others throughout the Island.[19]

One of the funeral expenses was the gravestone. Gravestone prices varied considerably depending on size and quality. Few stones provide such a definitive record as to their cost as the Lydia Benitt stone, Columbia, Connecticut, 1791, on which "Pr. 7 Dollars" is cut in large letters beneath the inscription. There are, however, on Long Island, certain stones which appear to bear the stonecutter's fee, though in a less visible manner. In western Suffolk, particularly in Huntington and Northport, are moderate- and small-sized sandstone death's head markers which appear to be cheap versions or copies of the gravestones carved by the Lamson brothers of Massachusetts. Set far below the inscriptions, often invisible unless a little digging is done, are sets of numbers. On the Sarah Higbee stone, Northport, 1759, is found this lightly incised notation: "00-14-6." In the same burying ground, on the Thomas Rogers stone, this sequence is cut: "1-6-6." These sets of numbers, positioned far enough down the stone to be ordinarily out of sight, strongly indicate they were currency notations arranged by the English system of pounds, shillings, pence. They parallel the prices Harriette Merrifield Forbes lists for average New England stones.[20] These prices are also within range of the £1, 6s average value the citizens of Huntington placed on the gravemarkers destroyed when British Col. Benjamin Thompson built a fort over the village burial grounds.[21]

The best written evidence for the cost of gravestones on Long Island is found in a letter dated March 12, 1761, sent from Boston by Henry Lloyd to his father, Henry Lloyd, Esquire, of Queens Village, now Lloyd's Neck. The Lloyds were one of Long Island's most influential and wealthy families, related by marriage to another of the Island's premier families, the Woolseys of Dosoris, now Glen Cove. While in Boston, young Henry commissioned several stones for his Woolsey relatives who died between 1759 and 1761. In his letter, Henry reported that he had ordered four gravestones with accompanying footstones (which still stand in the Woolsey burial ground). Among the four are the magnificent ministerial portrait stone of the Rev. Benjamin Woolsey, which Lloyd records as costing £8, 16s, 2p, the equally fine military symbol stone of Col. Melancthon Taylor Woolsey, which cost £6, 0s, 0d, and round winged death's head stones for the Reverend's wife, £2, 8s, 0d, and child, £1, 0s, 0d. Casing and "trucking" the stones were extra.[22]

The Distribution of Gravestones on Long Island

Long Island lies between two great centers of gravestone design and cutting, the earlier New England source and the later New York–New Jersey center of supply. In consequence of this, stones bearing the designs and motifs of both areas can be found on Long Island in numbers and mixes not to be duplicated elsewhere. Not suprisingly, Suffolk, which lay in a New England cultural zone until well into the eighteenth century, has the highest percentage of stones of New England origin. The western part of the island has a higher percentage of stones from the New York City area, and towards the middle of the island, in present-day Nassau and western Suffolk, mixtures of stones from both sources are common. However, grave markers cut by New York and New Jersey stonecutters are found as far east on the island as East Hampton and Southold, while stones of New England origin are to be found as far west as Jamaica. Certainly the greater number of Long Island gravestones are of New England provenance.[23] This is the result of three factors, one of which is the fact that the New England tradition was older and its practitioners larger in number. Second is the close ties maintained between the central and eastern Long Island towns and their spiritual homeland in New England. A last factor is the high attrition rate suffered by the colonial burial grounds in Brooklyn and Queens.

Types of Grave Markers

There were four types of grave markers used on Long Island. The first was the *tomb*, usually a rectangular brick vault, capped by a sandstone or slate slab on which was carved the deceased's name, rank in society, and exploits. Tombs are not common on Long Island and are largely confined to the North and South Forks, particularly Southold and East Hampton, though scattered examples can be found further west. This form of memorial was both elaborate and costly and was usually affordable only by those of higher rank and status.

Related to the tomb was the *table stone*, so called because its design resembles a table. It features several vertical columns, usually four, capped by a slab placed over the grave. This style is also rare, though a few examples can be found scattered across the Island.

Unmounted *grave slabs*, or *slab stones*, were also used. These are large slate or sandstone markers laid on the ground so as to entirely cover the grave. These, too, are not common anywhere on Long Island.

The most popular type of marker was the *headstone*, often paired with a somewhat smaller and plainer *footstone*. They were used by the thousands throughout New England and by the hundreds on Long Island (illus. p. 11).

The size of the early American gravestone varies greatly. Large stones stand in excess of five feet and can be nearly three feet wide. The average stone (not an easily determined designation) is about 3 feet by 1½ feet. "Small" could be anything below these dimensions. Since gravestone-making was a folk craft, there was no such thing as a standardized system of sizing stones.

The most common shape for the gravestone was the tripartite or three-lobed design which may have been established in the English colonies by the pioneer seventeenth-century American cutter known as the "Boston" or "Charlestown" cutter.[24] It is possible that the tripartite design was meant to represent a doorway and was hence symbolic of the grave's intermediate position between this world and the next. It has also been suggested that the headstone and footstone, resembling the headboard and footboard of a bed, served to emphasize the image of the grave as a place of rest.

While the three-lobed stone predominated, it was by no means the only style of grave marker used. Sometimes a simple round-topped stone was preferred, especially in the early period. For those who desired more ornate patterns, indented scroll-topped stones were fashioned, particularly by Connecticut Valley stonecutters in the post-1770 period.

The Gravestone Cutters

So completely did the American gravestone-cutting tradition succumb to social and religious changes in the first decades of the nineteenth century that even the native origin of the stones was soon forgotten. By 1900 it was widely believed that the seventeenth and eighteenth-century gravestones had been imported from England. Only with the pioneer researches of Harriette Merrifield Forbes in this century did the American origin of the colonial and early federal gravestones again become widely known. Forbes demonstrated the American provenance of the gravestones by first pointing out the absence of gravestones on English ship manifests of the period and, most importantly, by identifying colonial gravestone cutters. She accomplished this primarily through her researches into colonial probate records. By the time *Gravestones of Early New England* appeared in 1927, Forbes had identified 128 colonial gravestone carvers. Subsequent scholarship has increased that figure to 217, and further inquiry will probably lead to the identification of more.[25] Yet, even with increasing research, many gravestone cutters still remain unidentified. Many gravestone styles are immediately recognizable, and their artistic development and geographical limits are well-known, but their makers defy identification, and most likely always will.

The colonial gravestone carvers were frequently engaged in other trades besides cutting gravestones. Not surprisingly, many cutters labored in second occupations which also required skill in stonecutting. Even such well established gravestone carvers as the Stevens family of Newport, Rhode Island, and the Johnsons of Middletown, Connecticut, frequently undertook housebuilding and general masonry projects. Other stonecutters were cordwainers, shoemakers, carpenters, braziers, and ship captains.

Although second occupations were common, it seems clear that from the 1730's some gravestone cutters had become well enough established to concentrate on the crafting of gravestones and a few may have been able to do so exclusively. Entire families sometimes practiced the trade and an apprentice system is known to have existed or can be surmised for several workshops. The development of an apprentice system adds to the difficulty in identifying the carver of a stone since apprentices or sons (no women are known to have carved gravestones) commonly copied the style of their fathers or masters. Indeed, if the father's or master's style had become popular, and hence profitable, imitation was probably mandatory. Some styles became so popular that their influence can be seen in the work of many stonecutters other than the originator. Outright plagiarism, however, was rare. Attempts to identify a cutter by tracing stylistic progressions or delineating the career of a known gravestone cutter are sometimes complicated by several factors. These include the practices of stockpiling stones with the symbols completed but the inscriptions left blank, of trading or selling half-finished stones among cutters and inscription carvers, and of the ordering of replacement stones for worn-out, damaged, and perhaps unfashionable markers. Such common practices distorted the carvers' chronological sequences.

One of the great gaps in our knowledge of the colonial gravestone carver deals with the symbols they carved on the stones. We do not know from their own words what the symbols meant to them and where they got their ideas for the images they carved. Probate records, bills, letters, and even the few diaries that have survived provide little information in this regard. Probably it was obvious to both the gravestone carver and his customer what the symbols meant and there was no need to discuss it. Few of the cutters had any artistic pretensions, which is probably why it never occurred to them to put down in writing the sources of their inspiration. Fortunately, we can determine the meaning of the symbols and the sources of at least some of the designs through other means, but the lack of information in the carvers' own words is still missed.

Only one Long Island gravestone cutter who practiced during this period can be identified. This was Ithuel Hill who emigrated from Connecticut to eastern Suffolk and began to make gravestones at the very end of the eighteenth century. The lack of data on Long Island carvers may be largely a result of a paucity of surviving records. Since few stonecutters signed their work and colonial records are often sketchy, it is possible, though not probable, that there were other Long Island gravestone cutters whose names simply disappeared. More likely, because of the lack of suitable materials for gravestones and because the area is surrounded by two major centers of gravestone production, gravestone cutting was not economically viable on Long Island.

Materials of the Early American Gravestone

Materials most commonly used to fashion gravestones were slate and sandstone. Often the stone carvers received these materials already cut into blanks at the quarry, which enabled them to go right to work on the designs and inscriptions. Slate varied in color from near-black to greenish, with a light blue-grey shade predominating. Occasionally, slate is found streaked with other colors, most often white on Long Island. Sandstone also appears in several varieties varying in hue from deep brown to near-red. For cutting purposes, slate, being harder, took fine lines and incisions better than sandstone and was more suitable for fine detail. Sandstone, on the other hand, was easier to cut and lent itself to deeper and bolder carving. Sandstone of less than top quality does not wear as well as slate. Being grainier, it suffers from erosion and is frequently found in a disintegrating condition. This is particularly true of the common style of post-1780 soul effigy stones which appear to have been cut on sandstone inferior to that previously supplied. Slate can deteriorate as well, but its great enemy, besides people, is moss and lichen.

Other stone material such as granite and schist was sometimes used and, at the beginning of the period, local field stones served as well. Towards the end of the eighteenth century the soft white marble from Vermont, which came to dominate the nineteenth-century burying ground, began to see limited use. This marble wears very poorly, as anyone who has visited a graveyard containing these stones can attest. Frequently, eighteenth century and even seventeenth-century stones are quite well-preserved and legible while the designs and inscriptions on the nineteenth-century marbles are obliterated.

Headstones, footstones, and tombs at South End burial ground, East Hampton. Behind the brick tomb is a table stone, a rare style of grave marker on Long Island.

CHAPTER II

The Symbols of the Stones

Primary Symbols

SYMBOLS OF MORTALITY: THE WINGED DEATH'S HEAD

The death's-head symbol which was first carved in the Boston area as early as 1678 is found on Long Island with dates going back to 1687. The winged skull symbolized the transitory nature of earthly existence and the fleetness with which death overtakes all. It was a lesson to all who gazed upon it that the pleasures and glories of this life are temporary and the pursuit of earthly riches and fame at the expense of preparation for man's true end—salvation in the afterlife—is folly. The winged death's head was a reminder that none could escape the judgment of God. The death's-head stones so perfectly embodied these beliefs that the Puritan divine Cotton Mather referred to them in *Death Made Easie and Happy* when he enjoined the reader to remind himself daily "that he shall die shortly. Let us look upon everything as a sort of death's head set before us, with a memento moris written upon it."[26] A more positive interpretation holds that the winged death's head might also have looked forward in time to the Second Coming of Christ, when the bodies and souls of the just could be reunited in a glorified state and ascend to heaven. In this sense, it held out the hope of spiritual regeneration.[27]

The winged death's head was easily the most widely used mortality symbol, but it was not the only one. There are stones on which somber, wingless skulls and crossbones are cut. Crossbones also found their way onto stones alone. They can sometimes be found in smaller versions placed above the skull. The same is true of another symbol of passing time, the hourglass.

On some early stones, coffins and picks and shovels appear as secondary symbols on the borders, though the imps of death with their deadly darts found in New England did not make it across Long Island Sound.

The message of impending death was sometimes put into written form on the epitaphs which are frequently, but not always, found on early American gravestones. *Hora Fugit, Memento Mori* (the hour flies; remember you must die) is a common inscription found on many stones. Others are:

Death is the wages due to Sin
Through Christ eternal life we win
    Mary Smith, Nissequogue, 1766

The Clear delits wee here enjoy
We fondly call our own
But short favouer boured now
to be repaid on
    John Carman, 1759, Dix Hills

Her thread was short, her glass
Her sorrow o'er, her joy soon run
    Catherine Willet, 1749, Grace Church, Jamaica

This Life is a Dream
and an empty sho
Into the Wide World we must go
        Richard Lawrence, 1781, Lawrence Manor, Steinway

Behold and see as you pass by
As you are now so once was I
As I am now so you must be
Prepare for Death and follow me
        John Satterly, 1749/50, Old Huntington Burying Ground

The last epitaph, dating from the fourteenth century, was among the most popular of its type. It had a very wide distribution.

SYMBOLS OF RESURRECTION AND SALVATION:
THE WINGED SOUL EFFIGY

On Long Island and through most of New England, the winged death's head began to fall into disuse in the 1750's. Its last appearance is on the 1771 Sarah Ogden Van Cortland stone in Grace Churchyard, Jamaica. This harsh warning of death and judgment fell out of favor while symbols depicting the triumph of the soul and its glorification in heaven became the most popular funerary symbols until the nineteenth century.

Apparently, there were also attempts to fuse the death's head with a symbol for the soul in order to create an image showing the metamorphosis between physical death and the eternal life of the soul in heaven. Examples, however, are exceedingly rare on Long Island.

The soul effigy proper was carved almost as early as the winged death's head, and it survived into the early part of the nineteenth century. The soul effigy in its many guises appears as a face surrounded or supported by wings. For this reason the images are frequently called angels or cherubs. In fact, the stonecutter may have seen little difference between the glorified soul of the just and an angel. Some cutters, especially those along the coast who were influenced by the neoclassical revival of the eighteenth century, did carve symbols readily discernible as putti or cherubim. Indeed, such well-known and prolific gravestone cutters as John Stevens Jr. (III) and Henry Christian Geyer used the term cherubim themselves. Most symbologists, however, believe the face surrounded by wings was most often meant to represent the soul in heaven.

Because of its widespread and longstanding use, the soul effigy was the single most powerful symbol of salvation. As with the lesson of mortality, that of salvation was often verbalized in epitaphs on the stones:

Here lyes Elizabeth
Once Samuel Beebee's wife.
who once was made a living Soul
But now's deprived of life.
Yet firmly did believe
that at her Lord's return
She should be made a Living Soul
in his own shape and form
Liv'd four and thirty years a wife

was aged fifty-seven
Has now lay'd down her mortal Soul
In hopes to live in heaven.
June the 10th 1716
     Orient

In this epitaph the hope of salvation is blended with a strong reference to the Second Coming when body and soul will be reunited in glorified form — in Christ's "own shape and form."

Most of the salvation epitaphs are not as well developed theologically, but the essential message of salvation is clear.

> *Into thy Courts O Lord she fled*
> *Through the dark Mansions of the Dead*
> *In this thy palace now she's fixed*
> *In joys celestial and unmixt*
>   Joannah Willet, 1749, Grace Church, Jamaica

> *Eternal Bliss shall Innocence Enjoy*
> *And Endless pleasures which can never cloy*
> *While here Entombed a virtous youth doth Rest*
> *In certain hopes of being completely blest*
>   Elbert Willet, 1738, Grace Church, Jamaica

> *Her soul has now taken flight*
> *To mansions of glory above*
> *To mingle with angels of light*
> *and dwell in his kingdom of love*
>   Tabitha Taylor, 1822, South Commack

The Joanna Conkling stone, 1775, is an example of carved floral work.

SYMBOLS OF RESURRECTION AND REGENERATION:
FLOWERS, VINES, AND GOURDS

Flowers are an ancient symbol of regeneration and rebirth. Along with vines and floral scrollwork, flowers are common secondary motifs on early American stones, their symbolic function perhaps secondary in importance to their aesthetic appeal. Occasionally, however, they are given the spotlight as the central symbol on the tympanum. Two flower-engraved stones of the type cut by Ebenezer Price [p. 51] or one of his apprentices are found in the Wainscott burying ground. Both are identical but the Joanna Conkling stone, 1775, has survived time and weather better (illustrated). The flowers are cut in a balanced pattern in the rather bold style reminiscent of Pennsylvania Dutch art or the related art of the German settlements of southwest Virginia.[28] It must not be forgotten that flowers and vines, particularly in a subsidiary position, may have been selected solely for visual effect, setting off the centerpiece and increasing the aesthetic value of the entire stone.

On certain East End stones of New England origin, border symbols are encountered which may represent either gourds or female breasts. This erotic symbol may seem out of place on stones supplied to such Puritan communities, and perhaps they do represent a sublimated inclination towards sexuality, but the conscious symbolism was that the breasts

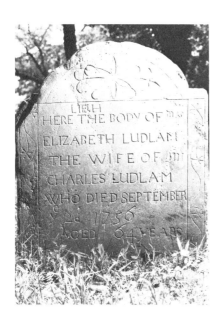

The star centrally placed on the Elizabeth Ludlam stone, 1756, replaces a soul effigy.

symbolized the teachings of the Church which was the milk which nourished the soul.

Secondary Symbols

THE CROWN OF RIGHTEOUSNESS

The major or central symbols on early American gravestones are to be found in the tympanum, the large section of the stone above the inscription. Secondary symbols sometimes compliment the central symbol itself or appear along the borders or on the border finials. Among the more widespread of these secondary symbols is the Crown of Righteousness, which is often worn by a soul effigy. Crowns come in all sizes and shapes: made of tulips, flowers, and feathers; various medieval-looking coronets; and some with billowing shapes, perhaps representing cloth-capped crowns. When found over a skull, a crown simply reemphasized the triumph of death. Over a soul effigy, it represented the Crown of Righteousness which the souls of the just wear in heaven as a sign of their resurrection in Christ.

SHELLS, PINWHEELS, AND ROSETTES

The shell, rarely found in the tympanum but occasionally seen on border finials, might represent life. It was also, however, a common furniture motif in the eighteenth century and might simply have been included for fashion or style. The same is also true of pinwheels and rosettes. The pinwheel, derived from an Etruscan and Roman funerary motif and usually found on border finials, may symbolize "the whole masse and body of all things under heaven, subject to continual change and mutation."[29] When placed centrally in the tympanum, as is sometimes seen, the pinwheel might have symbolized eternal life or taken the place of a soul effigy. Then again, the pinwheel, which appears on such mundane objects as watch boxes, often may have been only a pleasing stylistic flourish.

SUN, MOON, AND STARS

The sun, moon, and stars (among the most popular of secondary symbols) are sometimes used to frame soul effigies and can represent the timeless expanse of the universe. The great Puritan preacher Jonathon Edwards gave us another view when he wrote that these celestial bodies represent the different glories of Christ and the glorified saints.[30] Some difficulty may arise when trying to distinguish between pinwheels and stars, but in either case a general word of caution is in order. The very same type of stars and swirls cut into border finials can also be found on common colonial household objects such as tape looms.[31] There is, of course, no reason why the early American gravestone cutters might not have been combining both theological and artistic motivations when they chose these symbols, and the fact that such motifs merged spiritual and secular impulses might have made them all the more attractive.

Like pinwheels, stars sometimes replaced soul effigies. The only example of this primary use of a star on Long Island is on the gravestone of Elizabeth Ludlam, Center Island, 1756 (illustrated).

PORTRAIT SYMBOLS, OCCUPATIONAL SYMBOLS, AND COATS OF ARMS

Not all the symbols on stones of the 1660-1820 period were religious in their inspiration. From the very beginning, stones were cut whose only concern appeared to be to commemorate the individual buried beneath and which, therefore, are primarily biographical in nature. The most common of these are portrait stones of which there are several varieties, differentiated by medium, style, and degree of individualization of the portrait.

Gravestones bearing realistic portraits of the deceased are rare on Long Island. The finest examples of this type appeared in New England in the mid-eighteenth century and were usually used to mark the resting place of ministers. These New England stones not only demonstrate a high degree of technical proficiency but also show the stone carvers to have been abreast of the portrait-engraving styles used in eighteenth-century publications. The only extant example of New England-style portrait stone on Long Island is the beautiful pale-blue slate stone of the Rev. Benjamin Woolsey, 1759, Glen Cove (illustrated). Woolsey was born in Jamaica in 1714 and held a pastorate in Southold before moving to the little settlement of Dosoris in 1736. It was he, in fact, who gave the little community its name. Woolsey had married the heiress of one of the first settlers of the then independent settlement and in her honor called it Dosoris, the name being a corruption of the Latin *Dox uxoris*, or wife's dowry. The Reverend's stone is as exquisite as any found in New England. It presents the minister in full clerical garb looking at the viewer from a three-quarter profile. This stone stands in a row next to the equally fine stone of his son, Melancthon (see below), and his grandchildren's triple-cherub marker. In the lower left corner of the latter is the inscription, "Hemes, Boston." As all of these stones are carved from the same grade and color slate, cut in the same polished manner, and are separated by only a year or two, it is possible they are all the work of the same stonecutter. The signature probably stands for Henry Emmes, active in Boston and Newport from 1750-1790. However, the Reverend's marker is highly reminiscent of the work of another Boston carver, William Codner.

A rare realistic portrait on a Long Island gravestone appears on the Rev. Benjamin Woolsey stone, 1759. Less sophisticated is the portrait on the Mary Ann Tuthill stone, 1794.

A less sophisticated type of portrait appears on a number of small sandstone markers found in the Southold and Huntington burying grounds. In Southold are found the gravestones of Mary Ann Tuthill, 1794, and two other Tuthills who died in 1785 and 1790 (illustrated). The stones provide a full-faced portrait with naturalistic though identical features. These stones look, in fact, like wingless versions of the naturalistic common style post-revolutionary soul effigy.

Occupational symbols were also used on early American gravestones both as central and subordinate symbols. The occupational symbols most frequently found are those signifying military service. The single example of this type on Long Island is a magnificent slate from the previously mentioned Woolsey cemetery in Glen Cove. The stone, probably by William Codner, is a pale-blue slate on which is centered a beautifully carved medieval helmet flanked by various military accouterments: banners, swords, and clarions. This stone marks the resting place of Melancthon Woolsey, son of the Rev. Benjamin Woolsey (illus. p. 12). Melancthon served in the French and Indian War (1755-1763). He died in the first British attempt to capture the French Fort Carillon in 1758.

Coat-of-arms stones in the South End burying ground, Southampton: Col. Mathew Howell (above) and William Herrick (below).

Another type of stone celebrating the person rather than his fate is the coat-of-arms stone. Many modern Americans find it surprising that the early settlers from Europe erected gravestones cut with their families' coats of arms. The truth is that such stones were among the earliest carved by the New England stonecutters. English settlers who were entitled to display coats of arms exhibited them with pride. These stones, however, are more common in New England than on Long Island. The only coat-of-arms stones extant on Long Island are in the South Burying Ground in Southampton. Most authorities believe they were probably cut by James Stanclift I of Portland, Connecticut, though some feel they were cut by an unknown carver in the Windsor, Connecticut, area. These markers are large, pitted sandstones (though there is one modern granite stone nearby which replaces the original John Howell stone). The best carved coat of arms in that cemetery is on the Colonel Mathew Howell stone, 1706 (illustrated). On the center of this stone is a large shield with a strange lobed pattern on its top border containing the triple-rook arms of the Howells. In the same cemetery is another coat-of-arms stone cut by the same hand but in less well-preserved condition. This is the William Herrick stone, 1708 (illustrated). The coat of arms on this stone is badly weathered though it likely depicts a deer or horsehead within a shield.

MASONIC SYMBOLS

With many adherents among the infant republic's political and social elite, the Masonic Order grew in popularity at the close of the eighteenth century. Some Masons wished to commemorate their membership by having the order's insignia — calipers and all-seeing eye — engraved on their memorials. Masonic stones are not common on Long Island, and are spottily distributed. The best example is the Richard Floyd stone, 1803, Setauket (illus. p. 19), probably cut by Ithuel Hill. The use of masonic devices on gravestones ceased almost entirely after 1826 when a powerful anti-masonic political movement occurred.

THE CROSS

The universal symbol of Christianity, the cross, is conspicuous by its absence, unless we include minor subsidiary decoration. The cross was held by all the major Protestant sects of the seventeenth and eighteenth centuries to be a Roman Catholic symbol and as such was avoided. The first clear-cut use of the cross as a major funerary symbol on Long Island is found on the Ann Seabury stone, 1816, Caroline Churchyard, Setauket. The Seabury marker is closely followed in time and design by the Mary White stone, 1817, Grace Churchyard, Jamaica. The White stone itself is identical to that carved for John Ryan, 1796, Trinity Churchyard, Manhattan. Both the White and Ryan stones identify those interred beneath as ''inhabitant[s] of Ireland,'' and perhaps they, or their executors, were influenced by Catholic practice there. If so, the fears of the cross as a symbol of papist influence voiced by colonial Protestants had some justification. It is also noteworthy that these early cross memorials stand in the burial grounds of Episcopalian churches, a denomination whose many shared traditions with Roman Catholicism was a source of suspicion within the Calvinist churches.

It should be noted that none of the symbols described is specifically Calvinist, or even Christian. Most can be traced to antiquity. They were widely used and modified in European medieval funerary art, which was the form in which they were best known to Americans of the seventeenth and eighteenth centuries. The symbols were first carved on gravestones in Puritan New England but by the 1730s they were being freely used by stone carvers in New York, New Jersey, and points south — an unlikely development had the symbols represented only the Puritan view of death and salvation, as Anglicans and Baptists patronized these graveyards. Additionally, there was little sectarian bias in favor of any particular type of gravestone. Stones carved by the same cutters, emblazoned with the same symbols, can be found in Congregational, Presbyterian, Dutch Reformed, Baptist, and Episcopalian burial grounds. There exists, however, some evidence suggesting ethno-religious preferences for certain gravestone carvers. This widespread acceptance of the same or similar funerary symbols among the different sects underscores the fact that all these funerary images were derived from a commonly held European, perhaps Northern European, tradition of vernacular mortuary art which cut across denominational lines. The powerful religious impulse present in the early New England colonies may have been responsible for the earlier appearance of stones carved with symbols in that section of the colonies. It is likely that the New England example led to the development of a distinctive North American version of European funerary art.

The Richard Floyd stone, 1803, exemplifies the Masonic gravestone symbol.

A magnificent example of an occupational symbol is found on the Melancthon Taylor Woolsey stone, 1758. Woolsey served in the French and Indian War.

CHAPTER III

Gravestones of Long Island:
Plain Stones, Mortality Markers, Metamorphosis

Plain Stones

The earliest dated gravestone on Long Island is the sandstone slab which covers the tomb of William Wells, 1671, Southold, "Justice of the Peace and Sheriffe of Southold New Yorkshire Upon Long Island." The Wells stone probably originated in the Connecticut Valley. Most of the pre-1720 Connecticut Valley stones are unadorned, bearing only the deceased's name, birth and death dates, and less frequently, an epitaph or short biographical statement.

More typical of Connecticut Valley gravestones of the c.1670–1720 period is the Bethiah Gilbert stone, 1684, Southold (illustrated). This style of marker, with narrow stepped sides, broad-domed tympanum, and inside border was made by the so-called "Windsor Carvers" who were located in or near that Connecticut town. Most numerous, however, of all the gravestones carved by the first generation Connecticut Valley stonecutters are those crafted by James Stanclift I (d. October 3, 1712) and his son William (1687?–1761). As was true of almost all the early Connecticut and Boston stonecutters, the Stanclifts carved entirely with capital letters. James also favored a distinctive letter Ā with a bar across the top, and he can be further identified by his habit of putting periods after all or most of the words on the stone. James Stanclift is usually given credit for carving the striking Howell family coat-of-arms stones found in Southampton, but the body of his work is composed of plain inscribed stones. The Mr. Thomas James stone, 1696, East Hampton (illustrated) is a fine example of his work. James's son, William, continued to fashion stones after his father's style, though he favored rosettes in the pilaster finials and occasionally carved a very crude skull or soul effigy. The work of both Stanclifts is confined almost entirely to the North and South Forks; Southold contains all but one of the North Fork examples. Stanclift stones on the South Fork are distributed in the area between Southampton and East Hampton. Although gravestones patterned on these early examples are found with mid-eighteenth century dates, they are most numerous between 1684 and 1729.

Uninscribed stones arrived from Boston as well as from Connecticut and the second-earliest dated stone on Long Island is the small, thick, neatly engraved slate marker of Abigail Moore, 1682, Southold (illus. p. 22).

Plain but professionally engraved stones were produced throughout the entire colonial and early federal period. In the latter part of the eighteenth century, as the gravestone workshop tradition began to decay, plain markers with "In Memory" or "In Memorium" headings became increasingly common.

In the late seventeenth and early eighteenth centuries, homemade gravestones were carved in rural areas from local fieldstones. These were usually carved with initials, though sometimes with name and death dates. The Silas Sammis Stone, 1723, Huntington (illus. p. 22) is a fine example of this simple approach. As professionally carved gravestones became more widely available, these crude, uncommon markers fell into disuse, though they turn up as late as 1819.

The stepped sides, broad tympanum, and inside border of the Bethiah Gilbert stone, 1684, suggest Windsor, Connecticut origins while the style of lettering on the Thomas James stone, 1696, is distinctive of James Stanclift I.

Most of the early Massachusetts Bay stones are unadorned, like the Abigail Moore stone, 1682. The rough-hewn Silas Sammis stone, 1723, was probably made locally.

Closely related to the above, but a bit more ambitious, are gravestones produced by amateurs which bear not only inscriptions but attempts to duplicate the symbols found on professionally carved stones. One of the better examples of this type is the William Charles stone, 1718, Old Prospect Cemetery, Jamaica (illustrated). Here the amateur carver attempted to copy on the granite stone the fashion of the time by outlining a winged soul effigy capped by an overly large hourglass. Grave markers of this type are rare, and the only other examples in this category are found in the McCoun burial ground in Oyster Bay.

Mortality Markers

The earliest style of winged death's head on Long Island is found only in the North and South Forks and is of New England provenance. Some of these stones are the work of the greatest of the seventeenth and early eighteenth-century Boston stonecutters: the unidentified "Boston" or "Charlestown" stonecutter, William Mumford, and Nathaniel Emmes. These stones are small thick gray slates, usually two feet high. On these stones, skulls are frequently small in comparison to later styles and the borders are carved with elaborate designs, usually thick-leafed vegetation and gourds or breasts. Secondary mortality symbols such as picks and shovels or crossbones are also found in the border shoulders. The memorials of the "Boston Stonecutter," of William Mumford, and of Nathaniel Emmes are not always easy to distinguish. However, since the Stonecutter seems to have ceased work in 1695, and Mumford carved into the eighteenth century (he died in 1718), some attributions can be made. The earliest of these winged skulls is on the Mary Youngs stone, 1687, Southold (illustrated). It is one of the two Long Island stones which clearly fall within the known dates of the Stonecutter's activity.

An almost classic example of these early stones is the marker of Daniel Alsop, 1698, Southold (illustrated). This is an archaic-looking stone with a tiny skull and long wings. Note the pick and shovel on one border finial and the crossed bones on the other. These auxiliary symbols of mortality tended to fall into disuse after the first few years of the eighteenth century. The thick foliate-and-gourd borders are typical of the many stones cut at the turn of the seventeenth century. The Thomas Stephens stone, 1701, Southampton (illustrated), is another excellent example of an early death's head. This stone, probably cut by William Mumford, boasts another subsidiary mortality emblem, the hourglass, which is placed over the neatly carved skull. A border is cut below the skull itself, dividing the tympanum from the inscription. In this border, spiraling foliage supports a targetlike circle directly beneath the skull itself. The pilasters are cut with a thick leaf-and-vegetable motif, which is capped in the finials by a sunflower, a symbol of regeneration. This contrasts with the death's head in the tympanum.

Of special interest is the Samuel Hutchinson stone, 1717, Southold (illustrated). This small slate, probably carved by Nathaniel Emmes, is an example of what some authorities call "punning." The skull's wings are raised and shaped in such a way that they form a heart, cleverly juxtaposing life and death motifs.

With the death of Mumford in 1718, the first generation of Boston stone carvers came to an end. The men who replaced them began to carve stones

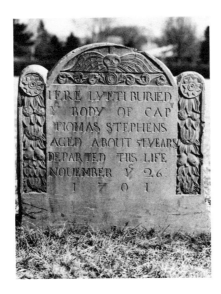

Clockwise from top left: The William Charles stone, 1718, is an amateur attempt to duplicate fashionable symbols. The Mary Youngs stone, 1687, with its winged death's head, originates in the Boston area. Two classic examples of early winged skulls are the Daniel Alsop stone, 1698, with auxiliary symbols on the border finials, and the Thomas Stephens stone, 1701, probably cut by William Mumford. The Samuel Hutchinson stone, probably carved by Nathaniel Emmes, has wings that form a heart around the skull. A childlike winged skull was cut by John Stevens I on the Hannah Tuthill stone, 1711.

Stones cut by the Lamson brothers: note the death's head on the Benjamin Reeve stone, 1740, and the soul effigy on the Edward Huntting stone, 1745.

in their own styles and usually on much larger slates.

There was, however, another stone carver at work in this early period who cut death's heads of a rather different type. The strange, childishly incised skull, with a suspended line of "hanging" teeth, which tops the Hannah Tuthill stone, 1711, Orient (illus. p. 23), was cut by John Stevens I, founding father of the famous Stevens family of Newport whose members were active and prominent throughout the entire eighteenth century and beyond. Stevens apparently learned stonecutting from William Mumford in Boston. He moved to Newport in 1705 where he established his shop.[32] His death's heads are crudely designed, standing in some contrast to the much better articulated pinwheel rosettes which line the borders of these stones like a row of snowflakes. The only place these stones are found on Long Island is the Brown's Hill burying ground in Orient.

The Lamson Family

Inextricably bound up with the history of the early American gravestone, and the winged death's head in particular, is the Lamson family of Charlestown, Massachusetts. The founder of this remarkable family of gravestone cutters, which continued in the trade until 1808, was Joseph Lamson. Joseph was born in Ipswich, Massachusetts, in 1658. He learned his craft from the "Stonecutter" but later developed a style of his own.

He preferred a rather heavy dark-gray slate on which he carved winged, squat, square-jawed death's hands in the shape of long isosceles triangles. He was equally fond of heavy, draperylike foliate work which, when carved along the inner borders of the tympanum, gave the effect of curtains shrouding the skull. The lower border of the tympanum tended to be cut with more conventional foliate motifs, or, on more expensive stones, with small figures, subsidiary symbols, or mottos. Lamson's border finials often bore targetlike concentric circles. Again, the pilasters could be cut with foliate designs, gourds, and flowers reminiscent of the "Stonecutter."

Joseph's sons, Nathaniel and Caleb, became even more successful than their father. They originally copied his style, and the Abigail Jessup stone, 1724, on Jessup's Neck in the beautiful Morton Wildlife Sanctuary, is probably an example of the early imitative phase of their work.

Nathaniel Lamson, who was born in 1693, and his brother Caleb, born in 1697, dominated gravestone cutting in Middlesex County, Massachusetts. They had a flourishing business with many other parts of New England, Long Island, and far-away South Carolina as well. After their initial phase, during which they copied their father's work, the brothers, whose styles were almost identical, went off in their own directions.

Eschewing both the heavy stone and heavy style of the elder Lamson, the two brothers cut death's heads with delicate, sharp, and highly refined features (Benjamin Reeve stone, 1740, Southold, illustrated). They also carved soul effigies (Doctor Edward Huntting, 1745, East Hampton, illustrated). Their work is immediately identifiable. A fundamental feature of their technique was the use of cursive motifs and curving lines which tended to give their work a sensual, almost erotic effect. They kept the long-winged, somewhat flat-topped skulls of the elder Lamson but gave them a sharper, lighter appearance, frequently curling the wings at the tips. Indeed, the sharpness of the cutting on the death's heads, with their villainous upturned "eyebrows," makes them more sinister than the skulls carved by their father or the "Stonecutter." The skulls also are more menacing than the more rounded variety which came into vogue towards the end of their careers. The skull is usually set off by narrow, curling, foliate designs, which frequently boast a flower or leaf in the center, surmounting the skull or at the bottom of the tympanum. Typically, the pilaster finials bear a rope-bordered circle in the center of which is an incised flower or leaf. The borders may be cut with more of the cursive foliage or with one of the distinctive hallmarks of a Lamson stone. One of their distinctive designs is a comma-shaped, swirllike leaf, not entirely unique to them. Another is what Mrs. Forbes dubbed the "Lamson device." This looks like a three-dimensional comma with an eyelet near the top. Quite possibly it was an evolution from the earlier gourd or breast symbol, or, as some authorities believe, from a fig pattern. Whatever its origin, its form was unique to the Lamsons, with the possible exception of one imitator. The device was also favored by the Lamsons as a footstone motif.

Gravestones definitely attributable to the Lamson brothers' workshop are numerous on the North and South Forks. In Nassau and western Suffolk there are a group of stones strongly reminiscent of the Lamsons' work except that they are carved on sandstone rather than streaked slate. These sandstone death's heads, which are confined to an area between Setauket and Sands Point, north of the Ronkonkoma moraine, can be divided into two types. The first are large stones, three to four feet in height, on which the caliber of the carving rivals that found on the Lamson brothers' slate stones. These stones are not common and tend to be clustered in the Sands family burial ground, Sands Point, and the Smith-Strong family burial ground, Strong's Neck, where the skulls seem more rounded than is usual in Lamson stones. Scattered examples can be found in Hempstead and Huntington. The second group are smaller, two- to three-foot, markers which are considerably less ornate than either the Lamsons' slate stones or the large sandstone markers. They bear only perfunctory scrollwork and a swirl in the pilaster finials, though their flattened skulls and arching "eyebrows" show their close relationship to the others (illustrated). Both types of sandstone markers utilize the "Lamson device" on footstones, the larger varieties sometimes having it on the borders as well.

These sandstone markers pose a problem in attribution. Some researchers think the sandstone death's heads are the Lamson brothers' work, but there are strong arguments for believing otherwise. Although the brothers may have carved some or all of the large varieties, such as the Robert Sands stone, 1735, Sands Point (illustrated); the smaller types lack the high level of craftsmanship characteristic of the Lamson workshop. Another factor working against a Lamson attribution is the total absence of the sandstone markers in the North and South Forks where the two brothers' slate stones abound. It makes no sense to believe that the inhabitants of the central sections of the island would have demanded that the Lamsons carve their gravestones from sandstone while their neighbors to the east received the same type in slate. Lastly, sandstone was not commonly used by Massachusetts Bay gravestone cutters who had no easy access to that material, while their region was rich in slate. The large number of surviving Lamson stones on Long Island and in New England show that the brothers worked almost exclusively in slate. It is true that the gravestone cutters traded different types of stone and occasionally carved their markers from atypical material, but not often. The large number of Lamson-like death's heads,

The Jerushate Chichester stone, 1742, and the Robert Sands stone, 1735, are both reminiscent of the Lamson style, though they may not have been carved by the brothers.

Rounded death's head stones include those of Peleg Potter, 1764, and John Wright (note the crossbones), 1749.

particularly of the small variety, precludes this explanation.

A possible solution to the puzzle presented by the appearance of Lamson-like winged death's heads in the central section of the Island may lie in the western Connecticut Valley. This sandstone-rich region was a major center of gravestone production throughout most of the 1680–1820 period. Gravestones were shipped in large numbers across the Sound. The location of the Lamson-like stones suggests that they were shipped from New Haven or some port to the west. Possibly, a Connecticut carver, noting the popularity of Lamson stones, simply began to carve copies. These may have been carved for a Long Island market — but not exclusively, as they appear in western Connecticut as well. The inhabitants of the East End, who had access to the genuine Lamson product, may not have found the sandstone versions appealing.

If these sandstone markers were not produced by the Lamsons, the failure of the Lamsons to extend their market to the west is puzzling. Conceivably, the additional cost of transporting the stones further west put them at a disadvantage with the Connecticut copies (if they were copies) in terms of price. Or perhaps their workshop was satisfied with the orders they were already taking and the brothers simply had no interest in expanding their market.

Lamson slate death's heads on Long Island bear dates from 1712 to 1756, with the largest number carved between 1730 and 1756. The large Lamson-style sandstone death's heads bear dates from 1735 to 1769; nine of the fourteen extant examples were carved in the 1730's and 1740's. The small Lamson-style stones are carved with dates ranging from 1742 to 1766 with the 1750's being the peak decade. The deaths of Nathaniel and Caleb, in 1755 and 1769 respectively, correspond with the demise of the winged death's head as a popular funerary motif. Their sons carried on the family trade but abandoned the distinctive style which made their fathers' work so striking and powerful.

The Rounded Death's-Head Stones

The less ornate, less menacing, rounded death's heads first carved in the Boston area may have been a late modification of the type of death's head cut by Mumford and his contemporaries. They began to appear on Long Island in the 1730's, and they grew increasingly numerous until the winged death's head disappeared around 1760. These stones tend to be about two and a half feet high and a bit over a foot wide. The death's head is round, smooth, and considerably less threatening than the Lamson-style skulls. The wings, too tend to arch in a gentle curve rather than thrusting out aggressively as they do on Lamson stones. The borders are usually quite narrow, with rudimentary scrollwork capped by two or three enclosed circles. These memorials are common from Oyster Bay east. The Peleg Potter stone, Huntington, 1764, is a typical stone of this type (illustrated).

Turned out in large numbers in simplified design, the rounded skull frequently shows a lack of originality in design and care in execution. The features of skulls of this type tend to be cut with a few basic strokes in a low relief. There are, as can be expected, a few stones which rise above the general level and catch the eye. The John Wright stone, 1749, Oyster Bay (illustrated), boasts an extra mortality symbol, crossbones carved over the skull. An even more striking example is the Hannah, John, and Bethiah

Hudson stone, 1754, Mattituck (illus. p. 28). This singular gravestone stands out not only because of its triptych-like shape, but because it provides such poignant evidence of the high rate of child mortality. These memorials were turned out by several Boston area stonecutting families, the Codners, Emmeses, and John Homer. Their markers are practically identical.

New York-Area Winged Death's-Head Stones

In Prospect Cemetery in Jamaica stand two squat gravestones which appear to be the typical rounded-skull type adapted from slate to sandstone. These stones mark the resting places of Nicholas Everet, Esquire, 1723, and his son, Nicolas Everet, 1731 (illus. p. 28). The markers are nearly identical, although the younger Everet's is slightly smaller and less ornate. No doubt the stones were cut by the same hand after the younger Everet's death. Where they were cut and by whom is difficult to ascertain. The style is that of the New England rounded skull, but there appears to be no other example of this type in sandstone. By 1730, New York-area cutters were beginning to meet the local demand for gravestones. All but three of the stones in this cemetery are definitely traceable to New York craftsmen. These reasons support a New York attribution for the Everet stones.

In the same cemetery are two other winged death's heads in sandstone which have no companions on Long Island. These are the gravestones of Dr. Israel Smith, 1734 (illus. p. 28), and Thomas Smith, 1723. The tympanum on each of these stones is smallish and the carving deep. The skull itself is not detailed, though it does present a somewhat wild-eyed appearance. A medieval-style crown over the skull symbolizes the triumph of death over life while heavy, blunt wings carry it quickly through time. A long, thick-stemmed, petaled flower appears in each border. At the very bottom of the Israel Smith marker, just where the stone is broken off, is the signature "Turner." Aside from cutting his name on this gravestone, Turner seems to have left no other trace of himself. This type of stone has also been reported in New Jersey. Its provenance seems to be the New York City area.

Yet another type of sandstone winged skull is typified by the Capt. Samuel Payton stone, 1740, St. George's Church, Hempstead (illus. p. 28). These stones, undoubtedly products of a lower Hudson workshop, range anywhere from one-and-one-half feet to three feet tall. They feature an outsized, heavy, square-jawed skull sometimes topped with a crown and supported by two high-arching, steep-sloping wings. The carving is bold and deep, and the overall impression is of massiveness. These stones are not very common but are distributed over a wide area from Jamaica to Sagaponack.

Skulls and Crossbones

While the winged death's head enjoyed wide currency from the late seventeenth to the mid-eighteenth century, plain skulls and crossbones, the ancient symbols of death, were infrequently used. Long Island boasts three types of plain skulls and crossbones. Two slate examples stand at opposite ends of the Island. The Abigail Mulford stone, 1764, East Hampton (illustrated), is a rough, thickish slate on which is carved a naturalistic skull in profile sitting over a pair of crossed bones. The second slate example is the

Plain skulls and crossbones appear on Abigail Mulford stone, 1764, and the the Sibil Thorne stone, 1759.

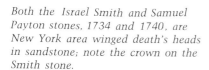

Both the Israel Smith and Samuel Payton stones, 1734 and 1740, are New York area winged death's heads in sandstone; note the crown on the Smith stone.

The rounded-skull stones of the Hudson children, 1754, illustrate the high rate of child mortality. The Everet stones, 1723 and 1731, a father-son pair, show the rounded skull adapted to sandstone.

Sibil Thorne stone, 1759, Sands Point, probably done by Henry Emmes (illus. p. 27). The Sibil Thorne stone is more ornate, carved in deep, three-dimensional, molded relief. It boasts an extended tympanum to accommodate the long skull.

The other style of plain death's head is represented by an identical pair of stones in north-central Suffolk and a marble version in Queens. The Mary Smith stone, 1767, Nissequogue (illustrated), is a brown sandstone marker bearing an incised skull with no lower jaw but with small pointed teeth. Behind the skull are two crossbones. About four miles from this stone in Smithtown is the Mary Arthur stone, 1766, which is identical but for inscription and epitaph.

The presence in the Lawrence cemetery in Steinway of the same symbol carved on the marble marker of Judith Lawrence, 1767, provides additional evidence that this style is of New York origin. More conclusively, the carver of this type of stone also fashioned the delicate pencil-sketch cherub stones (see pages 52, 53) which clearly emanate from the New York area. These two types of stones differ markedly in their symbols, but the stone carver's lettering, as well as his practice of only partially cutting through the stone between the tympanum and border finials, shows they were cut by the same carver.

Another mortality symbol which attained only limited use is the crossbones. A few individual gravestones of this type can be found from Sag Harbor to Oyster Bay with dates ranging from 1765 to 1773. The James Doughty stone, 1773, Oyster Bay (illustrated) is the most attractive of this variety on Long Island. This marker was also cut by the "pencil-sketch man."

The Decline of the Winged Death's-Head Stone

The popularity of the winged skull peaked in the 1750's after which, excepting such idiosyncratic areas as Cape Cod and Nantucket, it was chosen with ever-decreasing frequency. It was almost extinct by the end of that decade. The latest Lamson stone is dated 1756. The last of the small Lamson-like sandstones is dated 1764, and the last rounded-skull, slate type is dated 1771. The winged death's head was no longer popular in Boston by the mid-1750's, and allowing for a Long Island time lag, the demise of the winged death's head in the 1760's was to be expected.

It was not accidental that the winged death's head disappeared as a major funerary symbol after 1750. In the 1730's and 1740's, the English colonies were visited by a major religious revival known as the Great Awakening. The Great Awakening was a call for a return to religious belief which expressed itself in emotionally charged meetings, sermons, exhortations, and expressions of personal commitment. This emphasis on emotion and enthusiasm was in sharp contrast to the previous Puritan practice of quiet religious introspection and to the use, within the bounds of Calvinist theology, of reasoned argument.

By 1750 the Great Awakening was played out as an effective force in colonial life, but it had wrought a fundamental change in doctrine. Whereas it formerly was believed that no one could be certain of his or her salvation, after the Awakening a great optimism towards salvation took hold. This optimism led to the belief that certitude of one's salvation could be had in

Other stock mortality symbols include the death's head on the Mary Smith stone, 1767, and the crossbones on the James Doughty stone, 1773.

Two types of transitional symbols may be found in the heart-skull on the Manasseh Kempton stone, 1737, and the combination of natural and death's head features on the Thomas Watson stone, 1737.

this world, and that all were capable of achieving it. This new attitude can be seen in the admonition of Charles Chauncy, minister of Boston's First Church, to his congregation: "Be not discouraged, the Time of your Redemption draweth near. It will not be long before you will arrive at the Place of the *Dead in* CHRIST, where you shall eternally rest from all your Labours and Sorrows.[33]

This reflects a profound change in the attitude of Puritans and other sects towards death. Some even see in it the beginnings of a certain longing for death which later characterized the Romantic Period.[34] Certainly the change was reflected most visibly in churchyards where the winged death's head fell into disuse as a funerary symbol because it no longer accurately expressed the beliefs of the people.

The winged soul effigy, on the other hand, depicting the soul in bliss in heaven, was perfectly suited to the current needs of the populace. It is perhaps no coincidence that gravestones only become common on non-Puritan parts of the island and New York City after this change in symbols began to take place. While death's-head stones were carved by New York–New Jersey cutters, they are not numerous. This may reflect not only a lack of experienced stonecutters in the New York area before the 1730's, but also the unsuitability of such stones to the needs of the people. The soul effigy, borrowed from the Puritans and shaped into styles of their own choosing, was a symbol of spiritual hope, triumph, and optimism well suited to the needs of almost all Long Island's religious denominations, except the Quakers who eschewed ornamentation on gravestones.

Another possible cause of the demise of the winged-death's-head stones about 1750 was the growing prosperity experienced by the English colonies in the eighteenth century. With increasing power and prestige, the commercial classes may have resented a symbol that represented defeat, pain, and torment. The soul effigy was a symbol of success, and as such must have appealed to the inhabitants of the increasingly affluent colonies.

Stones of Transformation

Within the overlap of the two major funerary symbols of the 1660–1820 period, the winged death's head and the soul effigy, is a curious group of stones that seem to be attempting to depict the metamorphosis between the mortality of the body and the immortality of the soul. There are two variations of this attempt to depict the transitional state in the journey of the spirit into afterlife; both originate in New England and are rare on Long Island.

The first example of this type extant on Long Island is the Manasseh Kempton stone, 1737, Southampton (illustrated). On this slate, probably carved by Nathaniel Fuller of Plymouth County, Massachusetts,[35] we see an outlined head which, with the exception of the neck, bears a rather skull-like appearance. The eyes are empty sockets, the nose an open triangle, but where the teeth should be is placed a heart, the symbol of the soul in bliss or the soul's love for God. (Some New England examples show a diminutive human profile instead of a heart, as if the soul were escaping from the dead body.) The entire tympanum behind the head is cut with many slightly wavy, segmented lines representing a flutter of wings.

The second type of transitional stone does not attempt to depict metamorphosis on one stone. It was rather a sequence of stones cut in the

Connecticut Valley between c.1730 and c.1750 during which individual stones showed the transformation from death's head to soul effigy. The earliest stones bore plain death's heads; then some appeared whose images contained both skull and face characteristics. Finally, after 1740, all skull-like elements were abandoned. Two good examples of this sequence on Long Island are the Thomas Watson stone, 1737, Old Prospect Cemetery, Jamaica (illustrated), and the Phebee Gilbort stone, 1739, Southampton (illustrated). Both of these are cut on Connecticut Valley sandstone; both have thick floral border motifs utilizing flared wings behind their images — all features characteristic of the Connecticut Valley style of 1730–1770. The Watson stone, however, shows a face that bears the empty socketed eyes of the skull. The nose is cut naturally. Beneath the life-like nose are two lines which strongly hint of the grinning teeth that would be found on a death's-head stone. The Gilbort stone, dated only two years later, has a much more cheerful image with animated eyes while the mouth curves upward in a slight smile. All the characteristics of death have disappeared. In New England, these sequential stones were cut through the 1740's and 1750's, though by the end of the 1740's the transformation from death's head to soul effigy was largely complete. On Long Island, the depiction of the soul in metamorphosis is not common. Most of the Connecticut Valley flared-eared sandstones of this period show the soul effigy in its fully realized state. Perhaps the ambiguous nature of the transformational stone was confusing to many people who preferred their symbols to be unequivocal. It is equally possible that the change in religious belief concerning one's fate brought about by the Great Awakening had done its work.

On the Phebee Gilbort stone, 1739, all skull-like elements have been abandoned in favor of a cheerful soul image.

CHAPTER IV

Gravestones of Long Island:
New England Soul Effigies

The Connecticut Valley Flared-Ear Style, c.1740–c.1770

One of the great centers of gravestone production from the late seventeenth century until the old styles went out of fashion around 1815 was the Connecticut River Valley, especially the Middletown–Hartford area. The location of a large number of gravestone cutters in the valley was due, no doubt, to the easily exploitable sandstone with which the region abounds. Records indicate that several gravestone-cutting families, such as the Stanclifts, Johnsons, and Bucklands, either owned or had interests in the local sandstone quarries.

During the Great Awakening, the Connecticut Valley carvers worked through their skull-to-soul transitional stones and developed a pleasant-looking soul effigy, carved in shallow relief and supported by large wings flaring from the head in a manner reminiscent of an elephant's ears. The borders of the stones are usually cut with thick-leafed floral and foliage motifs.

Although several families carved soul effigies of this type, few were as prolific or as important in the development of popular styles as the Johnson family of Cromwell, near Middletown. The first Thomas Johnson (1690–1761) arrived in the area from New Haven and was carving gravestones before 1736. In the 1740's, he turned from death's heads to soul effigies. During this period he was joined in his craft by his son, Thomas II (1718–1774); the work of the two men is difficult to distinguish. They are probably responsible for the Phebee Gilbort stone and also the Desire Benjamin stone, Aquebogue, 1761 (illustrated). The Elizabeth Baker stone, 1753, East Hampton (illustrated), with its striking crown may also be an example of their work. It was the second and third Thomas Johnsons (1750–1789) who developed the elaborate Connecticut Valley ornamental style which took the region's gravestone-cutting tradition to a new height of design and technique before the old styles faded into oblivion at the beginning of the nineteenth century.

To confuse matters, there was an unrelated gravestone carver, Joseph Johnson (1698–1783?), working in East Hartford and Middletown who carved soul effigies similar to those of the Thomas Johnsons.[36]

By the 1770's, the flared-ear stones began to evolve into other styles largely due to the influence of Thomas Johnson II and III and Peter Buckland. On Long Island, the flared-ear stones have a wide range of distribution from Glen Cove to the Two Forks. They are not abundant but not rare, particularly on the East End.

The Stevens Family of Newport

Few families engaged in the gravestone-carving trade in the 1680–1810 period could rival the success — artistic and commercial — of the Stevens family of Newport, Rhode Island. The greatest of the Stevens family carvers were the first three Johns, father, son, and grandson, whose careers

Examples of work by Thomas Johnson I and his son are the Desire Benjamin stone, 1761, and the Elizabeth Baker stone, 1753.

correspond with the "classic" period of the American gravestone-cutting tradition.

The founder of the dynasty was John Stevens I, who left Oxfordshire, England, at the age of fifty and landed at Boston where he married a woman known only as "Marcy." While he lived in Boston, in 1702 his son, John Stevens II, was born. John Stevens I was a stonemason by trade, a builder of chimneys, cellars, and foundations. After he moved to Newport in 1705, he added to his skills that of gravestone cutter. Stevens cut death's heads (see page 13) and strange, sinister-looking soul effigies. On Long Island, these stones are entirely confined to the Brown's Hill Burial Ground in Orient.

The earliest dates of these soul effigies, and the earliest-dated soul effigy on the island, is the Gideon Youngs stone, 1699, certainly a backdated example. This weathered and partly broken stone utilizes curiously elongated breast/gourd symbols on the pilaster borders. A much better example of this type is the Sarah Paine stone, 1716 (illustrated). Here, the unpleasant, squared-off face born aloft by narrow wings, reminiscent of Royal Air Force insignia, can be seen more clearly. The borders are cut with an embryo-shaped, foliate design which terminates in a zinnia-like flower in the finial. The Abigail King stone, also 1716 (illustrated), is a smaller version of the same general pattern with the exception of a slightly open mouth from which it seems almost possible to hear a moan escaping. On the footstones which accompany these somber "cheroboam," as he referred to them in his day book,[37] John I frequently carved his idiosyncratic childlike death's heads.

John Stevens I cut one other style of soul effigy, much happier in appearance and fashioned in a more plastic, three-dimensional style. The only example of this pattern on Long Island is the Elizabeth Beebee stone, 1716, also found at Brown's Hill (illustrated). This stone, carved on black slate, is marred by broken border finials and deterioration of the face. Nevertheless, the essential features of this rounded-faced soul effigy can still be seen. The face is surrounded by twelve rolled curls and is carried aloft by two large wings. The lateral and bottom borders boast elaborate floral work with several stems and vines rolling up into sections which contain tulips or some other petaled flower. This type of stone bears a close resemblance to the John MacKintoshe stone, 1710, The Granary, Boston, which was carved by the Scottish immigrant gravestone cutter, James Gilchrist.

John I died in 1736 and the shop was taken over by John II who had probably been carrying most of the responsibility for some years previously. John II carved death's heads and soul effigies of his father's design, but went on to develop a soul effigy which proved so popular that it is the most common slate soul effigy found on Long Island. These soul effigies have an egg-shaped head flanked by two high, lurching wings. Typically, the eyes are narrow and slanted, and the mouth downturned, producing a most baleful expression. The pilaster borders are carved with thick scrollwork. The Hannah Townsend stone, 1740, Oyster Bay, is an excellent example of this type (illustrated).

The common pre-Revolutionary soul effigy — for this is what John II's effigies deserve to be called — exhibits little individuality other than the presence or lack of hair. On the Captain John Sands stone, 1712 (backdated), (illustrated), Stevens carved a soul effigy with hair combed forward in the Roman manner, a style greatly favored by his son. However, the usual John

The Sarah Paine stone, 1716, with soul effigy and embryo-like foliate design, was cut by John Stevens I.

Stones cut by the Stevens family, clockwise from top left: the Abigail King stone, 1716, with open-mouthed soul effigy; the Elizabeth Beebee stone, 1716, with elaborate floral work; the Hannah Townsend stone, 1740, with a baleful expression on the image; the Capt. John Sands stone, 1712, on which the hair is styled in Roman manner; the Nathaniel Smith stone, 1767, a conventional "haired" version; and the Samuel Huntting stone, 1773, which boasts an eighteenth-century wig.

The image on the well-preserved Esther Halliock stone, 1773, bears an expression of confidence. Note the detail on the stone's borders. The simpler Reve children stones, 1772, also bear decorated borders.

II "hair" model is capped by a ridge-shaped wig incised with swirls to depict locks and curls. The "haired" models also include eyelashes and eyebrows cut in the same fashion. A fine example of the wigged version is the Nathaniel Smith, Esq., stone, 1765, East Moriches (illus. p. 35). As might be expected, the stones carved with wigs and eyebrows also bear more ornate border work and are carved with thistles and acorns filling in the gaps in the scrollwork. Occasionally, John II's soul effigies are found with the wig, eyebrows, and eyelash ridges cut in outline but without the detail work of strands and striations. This usually occurs on smaller markers but can be seen most vividly on the Rev. Ebenezer White stone, 1756, in Sagaponack.

John Stevens II had a brother, William, who also carved gravestones. William's gravestones are similar to his brother's without being quite so rigidly stylized. The soul effigy is more naturalistic but without the refinements and detail that would appear in the carving of John Stevens III. William's stones resemble some of the soul effigies carved with hair and eyebrows in an unfilled outline.

The hairless soul effigy is the more common of John II's markers. Both varieties were carved in several sizes ranging from a little over two feet to more than four in length. Stevens's stones are well distributed all over eastern Suffolk. They thin out rapidly in the western sections and Nassau, and are represented by only one extant example in Queens. Dates of the common pre-Revolutionary soul effigy run between 1712 and 1775.

The enormous popularity of John Stevens II and other Rhode Island gravestone carvers was achieved largely at the expense of their fellow stonecutters in Massachusetts. John II's great commercial success was part of a larger economic transformation in which Newport took over much of Boston's Long Island Sound trade. This is clearly indicated by the precipitous decline in the number of Massachusetts gravestones erected on Long Island after 1760.

Of the three John Stevenses, it is the third who had the most pronounced artistic aspirations. He was the only one who signed his stones and the one we know most about. John Stevens III's artistic motivation is manifested by his attempts to integrate neo-classical influences coming from Europe into American craft patterns. Alan Ludwig believes John III was the first major stonecutter to use neo-classical symbols, which he probably adapted from engravings.[38] If so, this excellent cutter must bear the blame for introducing the bacillus which eventually destroyed the American gravestone-cutting tradition, though it is doubtful it could have been kept from taking hold anyway.

Known examples of Stevens's work date from 1769 to 1789 in New England; the Long Island dates of his work fall between 1770 and 1788. John III never carved mortality symbols, preferring to depict the soul in its glory. His images were frequently dressed in togas and often had their hair combed forward as in Roman portraiture. Carving on the blue-black slates his family received in undressed blanks from a nearby quarry, Stevens cut delicate, naturalistic portraits showing the effigy in three-quarter profile or full-faced. The relief is generally shallow, but the faces are well defined, allowing for full development of expression. The hair on the effigies, when not combed forward, is typically shown as curling locks falling down the side of the face. On some men's stones, such as the excellent Samuel Huntting stone, 1773 (illus. p. 35), eighteenth-century wigs are shown. The interior of the tympanum is sometimes cut with half-moon or rectangular devices, while borders were most frequently patterned with a thick-leafed, foliate design.

The best example of Stevens's work on Long Island, a stone which ranks with anything of his found elsewhere, is the often photographed and rubbed Esther Halliock stone, 1773, Mattituck (illustrated). The stone itself, a little better than three feet tall, is in excellent condition, being cut on the typical Stevens blue-black slate which seems darker than most. Centered inside the tympanum, which is bordered with a multi-rectangle pattern, is the three-quarter profile of the glorified soul of Esther Halliock, her hair arranged in flowing locks which fall along the side of the face. The expression is one of confident expectation as the face looks slightly upward and away from earth. The wings are full, well articulated, and so arranged that they seem to be pushing the soul towards heaven. The borders of the stone attest to Stevens's technical proficiency. The double lines which frame the inscription, dividing the writing from the pilasters, bulge with a half-circle on each side of the border. Inside the bulges are small circles in the center of which are Tudor rose-style flowers. The flowers are also found in the border finials and terminals. The remainder of the borders are cut with a checkerboard scroll pattern, while clearly incised at the bottom is the signature, "Cut by John Stevens, Junʳ."

Infant death was such a common occurrence in the eighteenth century, stones marking the common resting place of two or more childen are sometimes found. An example of such a memorial carved by Stevens can be found in the Presbyterian Church Cemetery in Southold. Here, rather than create a three-tympanum stone, as some stonecutters did, Stevens carved three small individual stones, putting his initials "JS" on only one. These three small stones mark the resting places of Kentury, Mary, and Abigail Reve who died between the third and the eighth of October, 1772 (illustrated). The hair ridges on these stones have no striations which may be due to their small size or to the fact that the stones were inexpensive. It is also possible that the plain ridge was meant to represent a baby's cap. The borders are carved with four petaled flowers and thistles incised with a cross-stitch pattern.

Stevens was a prolific cutter and is known to have advertised. An ad he placed in the *Newport Mercury* in 1781 boasts, "The stone in which he works is allowed by the best judges to be superior to any commonly found in America."[39] His commercial success as a cutter meant, however, that he had to turn out stones quickly. Consequently, visitors to the old burial grounds on the North and South Forks, where most of his stones are found, will soon come to detect what might be called the "stock" John Stevens III stone. These stones feature a full-faced soul effigy with shortish hair combed forward in the Roman manner. The borders are usually cut with a thick-leafed, foliate design (illustrated). Some authorities have sensed in Stevens the frustrations of a man who harbored artistic ambitions but whose commercial success prevented him from achieving it. Nevertheless, his accomplishments in the field of gravestone cutting places him in the highest echelon of those carvers whose identity is known.

John Stevens III had a son, Phillip, who carried on the family tradition of gravestone carving. However, Phillip abandoned the soul effigy styles his father had used and carved plain markers bearing only inscriptions. The Abigail Rhodes stone, 1806, Southampton, looks like his work. With that marker, the Long Island history of the Stevens Shop comes to an end.

The Zerviah Huntting stone, 1780, is an example of John Stevens III's "stock" pattern.

Clockwise from top left: John Bull's work resembles the Stevens style in the Easter Parsons stone, 1782, but diverges in the Conklings stone, 1778, where the images are highly stylized. Another Bull carving is the William Hedges stone, 1768. Typical of Benjamin Collins's work is the horrified effigy on the John Reynolds stone, 1750. The Nicoll Howell stone, 1760, is the work of Henry Christian Geyer, and the John Christopher stone, 1723, was carved by Lt. John Hartshorn.

John Bull

John Stevens III's great contemporary and competitor among the Newport gravestone cutters was John Bull (1734–1808). Bull does not seem to have matched Stevens in output, but he was willing to vary his style to a greater extent, producing three distinct types of stones. Most clearly related to John III's style is a type of curly-haired cherub or soul effigy like that found in Springs marking the burial place of Easter Parsons (illustrated). The image on these stones is identical with that on Bull's Langely children stone, 1786, Newport, which boasts six panels, each carved with the curly-haired cherub.

More distinctively in Bull's own style are the somber, majestic-looking soul effigies cut with deep, thick ridges around the eyes, eyebrows, and borders of wings. The Gilbert Conkling stone, 1776, Huntington, is a fine example of Bull's skill. Obviously the marker pleased the Conklings for Bull was later commissioned to carve the superb Philetus and Titu[s] Conkling stone, 1778, Huntington (illustrated). The soul effigy on the Gilbert Conkling stone is rendered in a double image with a common, though partly separated, third wing dividing the two images. The expression of other-wordly serenity and majesty is enhanced by the double image. Indeed, the twin soul effigies with their short, forward-combed hair, laced collars, and full, feathered wings are highly reminiscent of Byzantine angels and exemplify stylization in the best sense of the word.

The third type of gravestone attributed to John Bull found on Long Island, limited to the North and South Forks, is represented by the William Hedges stone, East Hampton, 1768 (illustrated). This depicts in three-quarter profile a somewhat dome-shaped head with heavy, sorrowful eyes, supported by a small collared neck. A large scythe cuts under the neck. It does not cut the hourglass in two as is sometimes the case on Rhode Island examples. Two small wings support the soul effigy.

Benjamin Collins

A Connecticut gravestone carver whose work on Long Island is extremely rare is Benjamin Collins of Lebanon, Connecticut. His only Long Island stone is the grave marker of John Reynolds, 1750, Glen Cove (illustrated). The stone is schist, incised and in low relief, and is cut with the typical Collins double-lined margins, simple vine and floral borderwork, and a strange soul effigy exhibiting a horrified, almost revolted, expression.

Henry Christian Geyer

Henry Christian Geyer of Boston was another New England stone carver whose work on Long Island is restricted to one example, the Nicoll Howell stone, 1764, in the Josiah Smith Burial Ground in East Moriches (illustrated).

Geyer, presumably of German ancestry, was fashioning gravestones at least as early as 1761 and was one of the more successful of Boston's gravestone cutters until his death in or before 1791. Geyer frequently advertised his services in newspapers, and perhaps it was through a Boston newspaper brought to Long Island that the Howells chose him to fashion this stone for their four-year-old son.

IV

The pagan-like image on the Joseph Baker stone, 1761, resembles designs from Anglo-Saxon England and Easter Island.

Lt. John Hartshorn(e)

On the East End of Long Island stand three primitive-looking soul effigy stones which are the work of Lt. John Hartshorn of Haverhill, Massachusetts, and Franklin, Connecticut. Forbes believed these stones to be the work of Joshua Hempstead of New London, Connecticut, but Ernest Caulfield, the dean of Connecticut gravestone historians, has challenged this earlier attribution and demonstrated that when Hempstead "wrote that he 'cut gravestones' he did not mean that he engraved designs on them. . . . The only obvious conclusion is that though he cut many inscriptions, Hempstead never designed a single headstone."[40] In other words, Hempstead was a middleman, buying the engraved but uninscribed stones direct from the gravestone cutters, and supplying the inscription whenever he received an order from a customer. The contention that Hartshorn, who was probably Hempstead's uncle, was the source of these stones is supported by an entry in Hempstead's diary for November 29, 1725. In this passage he describes buying gravestones from John Hartshorn for "woll."[41] Hempstead's diary is extremely valuable, for although he might never have carved the designs of the stones himself he was actively engaged in the trading and selling of gravestones and hence his entries tell a great deal about the economics of the craft. Barter was a common method of attaining gravestones and apparently Hempstead had a surplus of "woll" to trade. In addition to the above passage, he records another transaction in which he paid £10 worth of "woll" for eight or ten pairs of gravestones. At other times he switched from wool to bluefish, using a barrel or two as the medium of exchange.[42]

Of the three Hartshorn stones found on Long Island, the best example is the John Christopher stone, 1723, South End Cemetery, East Hampton (illus. p. 38). Christopher was returning home to New London from Martinique when the sloop on which he was sailing was wrecked off Long Island. His body washed ashore and he was buried in East Hampton. The stone is small and rough and cut in low relief. The major design is the most primitive of soul effigies, a small circle into which are cut yet smaller circles for the eyes and small straight lines for the nose and mouth. The entire tympanum is cut with antenna-like lines suggesting wings. The borders are carved with a series of double-lined, falling, comma-like patterns, while the finials bear encircled, double-lined quartrefoils. Another Hartshorn stone is in East Hampton, while the remaining example stands in Southold.

Other Pre-Revolutionary New England Soul Effigies

There exist many grave markers which defy easy categorization. One of the most striking of these is the primitively powerful memorial of Joseph Baker, 1761, Southold (illustrated). It is not exactly clear what this strange image is supposed to represent. There is some possibility that it represents a transitional skull-to-soul design, but this cannot be said with any certainty. Whatever it was meant to be, it is delightfully pagan-looking and resembles designs from both Anglo-Saxon England and Easter Island. There are only two other stones like it on Long Island. One is the stone of Ann Baker, Joseph's wife, which is next to his stone in Southold. The other is carved on the Joshua Wells footstone, 1761, Cutchogue. The Wells headstone is a fairly typical Connecticut Valley flared-ear or flared-wing stone, but the footstone shows a clear relationship to the Baker marker. The Wells footstone is slightly more elaborate than the Baker marker, however, with a low hanging curved line representing a jaw and a vertically cut ridge over the head which could stand for either a wig or a Crown of Righteousness. There is also some incised border work resembling vegetable stalks. The more elaborate design, while still intriguing, is less powerful than the Baker stone whose silent spectral image suspended between two swirls projects a most otherworldly and primeval effect.

CHAPTER V

Gravestones of Long Island:
New York–New Jersey Soul Effigies

The earliest dated gravestone carved by a New York–New Jersey area craftsman is the William Wells stone, 1696, Southold, which was probably cut by John Zuricher. This stone is clearly backdated as Zuricher did not launch his career until the 1740's, and it is doubtful there were many, if any, gravestone carvers at work in the New York region until the 1720's when winged death's heads began to appear (see page 13). It was not until the 1740's, however, that the New York–New Jersey school of gravestone carving really came into its own, a development which corresponds to the shift from the winged death's head to the soul effigy.

In contrast to those of New England, little is known of New York–New Jersey gravestone carvers. This lack of knowledge is partly due to the near monopoly New England has enjoyed on the attentions of researchers in the field. Another cause is the general paucity of surviving information concerning stonecutters in the lower Hudson Valley. Probate records which have proven successful in identifying many New England gravestone cutters have been generally unhelpful with the New York-New Jersey carvers. Nor have any stonecutters' diaries or account books of the period emerged. Newspapers have provided a bit more information — most of it tantalizing by its brevity. Between 1739 and 1771, New York newspapers carried advertisements by, or notices of, eleven stonecutters, six of whom clearly indicated they carved gravestones.[43] However, only three of these can be definitely credited with carving any surviving style of stone. To this list can be added four other gravestone carvers who are known by name, one of whom only by his surname.

While New York City-area gravestone carvers became every bit as proficient as their New England counterparts, they had a somewhat more limited repertoire and are generally more closely related stylistically. This is partly attributable to the smaller region they served, one which did not contain the extremes of distance, settlement, society, and raw materials, though it was ethnically and religiously more heterogeneous. Sandstone was the nearly universal medium used by the New York–New Jersey stonecutters, though a rare stone may be found cut from marble. Slate does not seem to have been used at all. The best sandstone apparently came from quarries in or near Newark. Although the styles of both known and unknown carvers in the region are clearly distinctive, several of the more important of them, such as John Zuricher and especially Uzal Ward and William Grant, show clear affinities.

On Long Island, New York–New Jersey carvers monopolize the burial grounds in Brooklyn and are responsible for all but two of the surviving stones in Queens. Their stones drop quickly in numbers in Nassau, but their work is found as far east as East Hampton and Southold, deep in the traditional strongholds of the New England carvers.

Our knowledge of the New York tradition of gravestone carving, particularly the quantity and regional density of their work, has been affected negatively by the process of urban expansion in New York City and its environs. Undoubtedly many more gravestones once existed in cemeteries which have been reduced to powder. The stones may linger out

V

An eccentric early Zuricher work is the Mery Gilford stone, 1755.

of sight beneath highways or playgrounds. Awareness of what has been lost should provide strong impetus for researching, recording, and preserving what remains.

The John Zuricher Workshop

From Brooklyn to Southold, though much more abundant on the western half of the Island, are a large group of stones that appear to be cut by the same hand or workshop. These stones, particularly those cut after 1759, are clearly attributable to one of the master New York City gravestone cutters, John Zuricher. The other earlier stones, bearing dates in the 1740's and 1750's, are similar, yet do not quite have the assuredness of technique and consistent polished look of the known Zuricher stones.

John Zuricher is known to have been active from 1749 to 1778, though 1777 is the latest date for a stone cut by him on Long Island. However, if the cutter of the 1740–1759 stones was indeed Zuricher, the William Wells stone, 1696, Southold (illustrated), the earliest dated stone carved in this style, is his. The 1696 date is clearly backdated. The difference between the stones cut before and after 1759 is enough to suggest that in the case of the earlier stones we are dealing with a younger, less assured Zuricher who had not yet fully realized his style. It remains possible, however, that the earlier stones were cut by another, older stonecutter from whom Zuricher learned his trade and on whose style he built his own.

The earlier, or proto-Zuricher, style is found on stones bearing dates from 1696 to 1765. The 1765 stone falls well within Zuricher's known period of activity, lending credence to the belief that all these stones were cut by him. In size, these stones vary from average to quite large, one being at least four feet tall. The stones depict a soul effigy, usually rectangular or pear-shaped, with thick eyebrows and a dipping, sometimes pointed chin. Hair is usually shown as a striated or rolled ridge. An exception to this usual rendition is the Daniel Youngs stone, 1755, Jamesport, which is bald (illustrated), a pattern Zuricher never repeated. The wings tend to arch high on top and curve upwards towards the center at the bottom, their feathers separated by half-moon cuts. The soul effigy is most often crowned, the crowns themselves showing a good deal of variation. The gravestone of Hannah Alsop, 1757, Long Island City, bears a fluted crown, while the Cathrin Clowes stone, 1740, Christ Church, Jamaica (illustrated), features a medieval-looking coronet. Yet another crown is featured on the Phebe Smith stone, South Huntington, 1760 (illustrated).

Two favorite flourishes found on these proto-Zuricher stones are the lines which extend from the end of the wings to the border finials where they are turned into spirals, and the placing of a wedge-shaped line at the end of the inscription. There is considerable variation in the facial expression of these stones. The Alsop stone looks cheerful, the Clowes stone serene, and the Wells stone bears a slightly astonished expression. Some of these stones have a wild-eyed, rather mad look, as on the Joseph Clowes stone, 1755, Christ Church, Jamaica.

The most eccentric of all the proto-Zuricher stones on Long Island is the memorial of Mery Gilford, 1755, Sands Point (illustrated). The stone's outline forms an unusual double finial flanking both sides of the tympanum. Typical Zuricher-style curlicues stretch from the effigy to the interior finials, while a star is carved in the outer finial. A slightly tipsy

Clockwise from top left, gravestones by John Zuricher: the William Wells Stone, 1696, clearly backdated; the Daniel Youngs stone, 1755, an unusual bald image; the crowned Phebe Smith stone, 1760; the John Lawrence stone, 1765, a fine example of Zuricher's work; the Cathrin Clowes stone, 1740, featuring a medieval coronet.

V

The scroll-topped Mehitabel Mackie stone, 1771, and the Dutch-language Jannitie Wyckof stone, 1774, are examples of Zuricher's later work.

crown hovers over a soul effigy which is topped with a flat, bristly wig which bears a striking resemblance to a crew cut. Spelling on the inscription is the worst found on any Zuricher or proto-Zuricher stone. Even though the cutter over-carved his spelling of February, he still did not get it right. The footstone is a smaller, simplified version of the headstone, featuring a scaled-down soul effigy, the only such example found on any Zuricher-type stone.

One of the finest examples of John Zuricher's carving is the John Lawrence stone, 1765, Lawrence Manor, Steinway (illus. p. 45). The stone itself is quite large and is of much finer quality than any of the stones previously discussed. It has characteristics of both the pre- and post-1759 Zuricher stones. The wings arch as on earlier stones, but the lines of the face bear close resemblance to the later varieties. The features of the face are delicately molded and more naturalistic than the faces typical of Zuricher's later work. The carving was executed with a delicacy of touch which serves to imbue the image with an aura of power, serenity, and majesty. The ridged hairpiece contains two sets of three interconnected spiraling curls reminiscent of Celtic La Tène art. The entire effigy is capped with a plumed tulip crown. The secondary decoration on the tympanum and borders is a sharp yet light foliate work more delicate than anything else Zuricher ever cut.

Stones definitely attributable to Zuricher can be identified not only by their style but also by the fact that he frequently signed them after 1759. Usually the signature is near the ground line and reads "John Zuricher Stone Cutter," though some stones in Brooklyn have "John Zuricher" carved on their backs. An excellent example of Zuricher's work in the final phase of his career is the scroll-topped marker of Mehitabel Mackie, 1771, Southampton (illustrated).

Zuricher was at home in both of western Long Island's cultures, English and Dutch, though records indicate he was a member of the Dutch community. He was capable of carving inscriptions in both languages; his gravestones in the Flatlands Reformed Church Burying Grounds being entirely in Dutch, which was a living language in the New York City–Hudson Valley area well into the nineteenth century. A Dutch-language example of Zuricher's more common-style gravestone is the Jannitie Wyckof stone, Flatlands Reformed Church, Brooklyn, 1774 (illustrated). This small stone bears the flat, two-dimensional image which was carved by Zuricher on his smaller and obviously less expensive creations.

As is frequently the case with identified stonecutters, little is known of Zuricher's life. There are several entries in the baptismal records of the Reformed Dutch Church in New York City of a Johannes Zuricher who was married to Elisabeth Ensler, sometimes spelled Anslar, Eensler, Insler, or Inslaar. His name also appears occasionally in newspapers or legal documents. As the name Zuricher was and is quite rare, there is little doubt that these references are all to the stonecutter. In fact, some of the newspaper articles identify him as such. Surviving records indicate that Zuricher had ten children.

John Zuricher's last years are as poorly documented as his early career. The dates on his surviving gravestones testify that he and his workshop (as it is hard to imagine how one man could have produced so many markers) were active until 1776. After that date his output plummeted to eleven markers bearing dates 1776–77 and only one memorial inscribed 1778. Circumstantial evidence suggests his career was interrupted, and perhaps terminated, by the British occupation of New York City which began in September, 1776. Zuricher was still residing, and apparently still working, in the city in the spring of 1776 when he was listed among those inhabitants whose windowpane leads were taken for use as bullets by the Continental Army.[44] No evidence has come to light concerning his movements between 1776 and 1781 when he was residing on the farm of his son, Lodwick, in the Haverstraw Precinct of Orange (now Rockland) County.[45] It may be that the few 1776–78 stones were carved there. In that year, stating he was "Weak and infirm in Body but of Sound and perfect mind and Memory," Zuricher made out his will. Among the possessions he listed were two lots in New York City described only as bounded by the Hudson River. Presumably, this was where his house and workshop stood. Zuricher died in May, 1784. The exact date has not been recorded, though his will was probated on the twenty-fourth of that month. Nor has the gravestone of this master of the craft been located. Yet he had not forgotten his trade and where his genius lay. In his will he described himself as "... John Zuricher now resident in Haverstraw Precinct Orange County and State of New York Stone-cutter ..."[46]

The Jamaica Style

The next group of stones under consideration were cut by an unidentified carver whose work is found in Manhattan, New Jersey, and Long Island. However, since six of the eleven stones of this type found on Long Island are either in the Old Prospect Cemetery or Grace Church Burial Grounds, both in Jamaica, it is convenient to refer to the group as the Jamaica style.

Though the earliest dated stone of this group, the Freelove Wilmot stone, Oyster Bay, bears the year 1735, it was not, in fact, carved until 1744 at the earliest. This is proven by the provision in the will of Freelove's husband, the Rev. Walter Wilmot, Pastor of the Presbyterian Church in Jamaica, dated July 31, 1744, six days before his death. It reads:

I do order that my Executors shall Procure
and Cause to be set up at the Head of my
Deceased wife's grave at oysterbay, one
toomb stone with this inscription to wit.
Behold my Dearest part has left the world,
Till nature into Ruines shall be Hurld:
Then, shall she rise Bright as the Morning Star,
and gain the Skies with Joyes beyond Compare.[47]

After the Reverend's death, gravestones were made for both him and his wife, and the Reverend's epitaph for Freelove can still be read on her stone which overlooks the Mill Pond in Oyster Bay (illustrated). Walter Wilmot's stone is found in the Old Prospect Cemetery in Jamaica which was originally a Presbyterian burial ground. Both Walter and Freelove's stones are identical, no doubt carved at the same time after the Reverend's death. The two markers illustrate the essential characteristics of the Jamaica style: a low-relief soul effigy with carefully cut eyes and eyebrows and a downturned mouth. The oval face ends in a small pointed chin, while the hair is shaped into a series of striated balls. The wings arch slightly and, on the Wilmot stones, the bottom arches of the wings double as a border for the

The Freelove Wilmot stone, 1734, illustrates the typical Jamaica-style soul effigy.

The Elbert Willet stone, 1738, and the Anne Carle stone, 1751, resemble the Wilmot stones.

inscription panel. The ends of the wings wrap up in the border finials where they are transformed into spirals.

Although the creator of the Jamaica style was quite capable of varying his soul effigies and accompanying ornamentation, his style was fixed enough that the relationship between them is never hidden. The Elbert Willet stone, Christ Church, Jamaica, 1738 (illustrated), bears a soul effigy that looks like a slightly puffier version of the Wilmot stones. Otherwise the expression is much the same. Note particularly the cut of the eyes on all the stones under discussion. The pupils are always carefully included, and little lines are incised on each side of the eyeballs themselves, lengthening them and giving them a slightly more animated appearance. On this stone, as well as on the others in Jamaica, the Wilmot stone excepted, the bottom arch of the wings is missing as is the spiraling of the wing lines where they terminate.

Closely related to the Wilmot stones is the Anne Carle stone, Old Prospect, Jamaica, 1751 (illustrated). It has the low-relief style of soul effigy of the Wilmot examples but with the small, neat, non-spiraling wings of the Elbert Willet stone. The presence of border designs differentiates this stone from all the others. The borders are cut with the bull's eye and scrollwork common on Boston death's-head stones of the same period.

In addition to their appearance at Trinity Church and in New Jersey, another clue that the creator of the Jamaica style was located in the city area can be found on the Abraham Lott stone, Dutch Reformed Church, Brooklyn, 1754. The stone is in Dutch, a language not often found beyond present-day Queens County. No stones in Dutch seem to be extant outside the city counties.

The year 1754 seems to be the end of the line for the Jamaica style. Lott's stone is the latest dated example still standing. The stonecarver either died, moved, or went into retirement, leaving only his gravestones as a testimony to his skill and creativity.

Uzal Ward

Uzal Ward of Newark (1726?–July 15, 1793?) was the most successful and prolific of the New Jersey stonecutters whose work is found on Long Island. Ward carved markers in two related but distinctive styles. The first, apparently earlier variation can be seen on the Nehemiah Smith stone, 1750, Old Prospect Cemetery, Jamaica (illustrated). This memorial features a square-jawed soul effigy with a striated ridge of a wig. The wings are narrow and rise up sharply from the chin. Two hourglasses flank the face but are separated from the main symbol by small petaled flowers. Springing from the hourglasses are two thick vines which are separated from each other at the top of the tympanum by an eight-pointed star resting on a disk. The design of these earlier Ward stones provides a striking juxtaposition of mortality and resurrection symbols. Only two examples of this style remain on Long Island, the Smith marker and the memorial of Henry Ludlam, 1752, also located in the Old Prospect Cemetery and unfortunately broken. Both of these are nearly identical to the William Bradford stone, 1752, formerly in Trinity Churchyard but now held by the New-York Historical Society. Signed by Ward, the Bradford stone makes positive attribution of this style possible.

Ward's later, more common pattern is dominated by a pear-shaped soul effigy with his typical long, thin nose and either striated balls of hair or, more commonly, an incised ridge for a wig. A tulip crown is ordinarily placed over the effigy. The soul effigy and crown are fashioned in strong relief using simple, bold lines. The inscriptions are in Ward's exquisitely fashioned lettering characterized by the lithe and attenuated "L's" and "Y's" with tucked-under swashes, and by the gently curving serifs on the other letters.

Nine of Ward's stones in the second pattern remain on Long Island. They bear dates between 1751 and 1774. A fine example of this pattern is the Daniel Smith marker, 1763, Nissequogue (illustrated). Emblazoned beneath the inscription is the carver's proud boast, "Cut by Uzal Ward at Newark." A slight variation of this style can be found on the Sarah Banks stone, 1764, Christ Churchyard, Jamaica (illus. p. 50). While the soul effigy is essentially the same as that found on the Smith stone, Ward has extended and rolled the wing tips into border finials, using the arch at the bottom of the wings to produce a scroll or heart effect. This marker is also signed.

Ward worked with sandstone obtained from a Newark quarry owned originally by Samuel Medlis. This particular sandstone seems to have been highly regarded throughout the region, and Ward stressed its provenance in an advertisement which he placed in the *New York Gazette and Weekly Mercury*, April 8, 1771.[48] The fame of the Newark sandstone was justified, as Ward's gravestones are in generally fine condition wherever found today. The advertisement also indicates that Ward had several men working for him at the quarry, though what part, if any, they took in the manufacture of his markers is not known. Ward also emphasized the speed and convenience with which he could deliver his stone, much of it intended for building construction from the tone of the ad, due to the "two boats constantly plying between New York and Newark."[49] Ward may have had a second occupation, not unusual for a gravestone cutter, as the New Jersey Historical Society has a record of an Uzal Ward who was named overseer of highways on March 13, 1764, and again on March 10, 1767. Ward resigned the post on August 4, 1787.[50] The first two dates fall well within the known range of Ward's activities.

The "Old Settler's Crypt" in Newark contains gravestones and bones removed from the Old Newark burial ground in 1887. Among the gravestones placed there is the memorial of Major Uzal Ward who died July 15, 1793, at age sixty-seven.[51] The rank indicates miltia or Revolutionary War service. It is doubtful whether Ward could have retained his post as Overseer of Highways after 1776 had he not espoused the Revolutionary cause. It is probable Major Ward and the stonecutter are the same. Ward was married at least once. The records of Newark coffin maker Capt. Robert Nichols contain the entry: "July 1, 1767 Uzal Ward's wife."[52] Should her gravestone survive and be located, it would be interesting to see if she was buried beneath one of her husband's markers.

In the churchyard of St. George's Church in Hempstead stands a gravestone which also seems to have had its origin in New Jersey and which shows the influence of Ward's style, but is not by him. This is the marker of Dr. Adam Seabury, 1800 (illus. p. 50). The soul effigy differs from Ward's in the almond eyes and broader nose, which gives the effigy a more disapproving expression than Ward's markers and is also cut in a plainer and less polished manner. The lettering, too, lacks the sharpness and flourish Ward

Uzal Ward's two styles are apparent on the Nehemiah Smith stone, 1750, which juxtaposes mortality and resurrection symbols, and the later Daniel Smith stone, 1763, dominated by a pear-shaped soul effigy.

A comparison between the Sarah Banks stone, 1763, and the Adam Seabury stone, 1800, shows the influence of Ward on his successors.

The Nathan Conkling stone, 1776, was cut by the Price workshop.

brought to his work. It is possible that this type of stone, fairly common in some New Jersey burying grounds, was carved by an heir or former apprentice of Ward's who took his general pattern but could not match his skill. It is also possible that this style of stone was cut by William Grant or someone working with him. Grant's style closely resembles Ward's in many respects.

Ebenezer Price and His Workshop

One of the most successful gravestone cutters of the second half of the eighteenth century was Ebenezer Price of Elizabethtown (now Elizabeth), New Jersey. Price (1728–1788) was not only an active cutter himself but also employed several apprentices, Abner Stewart, David Jeffries, and J. Acken, who all cut in styles highly imitative of his own. Many early New Jersey families had emigrated from Long Island, and the Price family itself had come from East Hampton. Whether or not they maintained any ties to that East End community is not known, but it remains a fact that Price's work leaps over Manhattan and the western and central parts of the island and appears only on the South Fork. A fine example of Price's work is the Abigail Howell stone, Southampton, 1771 (illustrated). The tight-mouthed, full-cheeked soul effigy was almost a patented device of Price's. Also typical was the rolled wig which terminates in small spheres. The outsized wings fill almost the entire tympanum, projecting a sense of power capable of thrusting the soul into the sky at a second's notice. Above the effigy itself is a device which appears to be a small cloud, perhaps helping to locate the current abode of the soul. The shell, a popular design in the eighteenth century, was favored by Price. Such symbols top both borders, one of which is unfortunately broken. The scalloped tympanum configuration is another characteristic of a Price workshop stone. Price and his apprentices also devised what might be called their workshop logo: incised crossbones which appear frequently at the bottom of their stones. Price and his assistants sometimes substituted a hand with a finger pointing to their names, a common advertising device of the time. A signature was frequently carved below the crossbones.

A short distance from Southampton, in Wainscott is the Nathan Conkling stone, 1776 (illustrated). Although smaller and less finely done, it is easily identifiable as the work of the Price workshop. In the same burying grounds are two examples of Price's less frequently used floral design (see page 15).

William Grant

William Grant arrived in New York from Boston around 1740 and began to advertise himself as a stonecutter, more specifically, one who "makes all sorts of Tomb-Stones and Head Stones."[53] His shop was apparently close to Trinity Church, and he directed all potential customers to get in touch with him through John Welsh, Trinity's sexton. In 1745 he was still in the same place but had taken on a partner, one Samuel Hunterdon, "Quarrier of Newark, lately arrived from England."[54] Evidently, Hunterdon supplied the stone, perhaps already cut into blanks, and Grant carved the symbols and

The Abigail Howell stone, 1771, displays the powerful winged soul effigy characteristic of Ebenezer Price's work, while the heart-shaped inscription on the Jonathan Cook stone, 1754, was created by William Grant.

V

inscriptions. Whatever style Grant was using in Boston, his New York stones closely resemble those of Zuricher and especially Ward. They are recognizable as the work of a different cutter in several respects, not the least of which is the fact that they lack Zuricher's assuredness and Ward's serenity. The best example of his work on Long Island is the Jonathan Cook stone, 1754, Quogue, (illus. p. 51) which he signed at the bottom. On this marker Grant positioned his soul effigy above a heart-shaped inscription area using a vine motif to fill in the space between the heart and the edges of the stone. Next to the Jonathan Cook stone stands that of Daniel Cook, 1774, a scaled-down, inexpensive version of the aforementioned marker.

Grant's work is not common on Long Island and seems totally confined to the southern East End. Possibly before leaving Boston, Grant had business contacts with the inhabitants of that area who maintained their loyalty after his move to New York.

Unattributed New York-Area Gravestones

THE PENCIL-SKETCH MAN

One of the most visually pleasing of all the New York gravestone styles is the unattributed cherub with closed eyes, pursed lips, and curling locks, exemplified by the Elizabeth Wright stone, Oyster Bay, 1755 (illustrated). The cherub is lightly incised on the stone, in an almost pencil-sketch style of cutting, resulting in a pleasingly idealized portrait of a sleeping child. The wings are pointed at the arch and tips, producing a genuine feathery effect. The Wright stone is an example of backdating because it was not erected until 1769.[54]

There are several examples of this style done in a larger and more elaborate fashion with the incised pattern rendered in relief. The best examples are found in the private burying grounds of wealthy families. In the "Tangier" Smith burying grounds in Strong's Neck where the Lords of the Manor of St. George are buried stand the stones of Henry and Margaret Smith. The Henry Smith stone, 1766, is essentially the incised pattern cut in a low relief with the addition of two daisies on the border finials. The Margaret Smith stone, 1764 (illustrated) offers a slight variation of the usual cherub wearing an atypical headband.

Another fine example of these stones is found in the Hewlett burial plot now in All Saints Churchyard, Great Neck. This is the well-preserved 1773 stone of Helena Hewlett (illustrated). While not quite as tall as the Smith stones, which stand about four feet, it shares their deep relief and clarity and detail of image. The Hewlett marker is one of the two on Long Island which bear a crown, and it is by far the finer stone. Examples of this style of stone bearing Dutch inscriptions can be found in the Gravesend burial ground in Brooklyn.

The anonymous pencil-sketch man also produced distinctive sharp-toothed skulls and crossbones (illus. p. 29). On Long Island and Manhattan his cherubs are more common than his mortality symbols. They are not numerous, however, though they do have a wide range. Two are located in Brooklyn, four in Queens, two in Nassau, and five in Suffolk. The dates of the stones run from 1755 to 1770. Recent research indicates that the pencil-sketch man was Thomas Brown of New York City.

The cherub on the Elizabeth Wright stone, 1755, resembles a sleeping child.

The Margaret Smith and Helena Hewlett stones, 1764 and 1773, share the clearly incised low-relief versions of the usual "pencil-sketch" pattern.

The unattributed Antie Wickof
Schenck stone, 1766, bears a simple
oval head surrounded by halo or wig.

The Damaris Ludlow stone, 1767, features a distinctively Oriental effigy.

The Antie Wickof Schenck stone, Flatlands Reformed Church, Brooklyn, 1766 (illustrated), is another unattributed soul effigy peculiar to the New York City area. The stone bears a simple molded oval for a head which in turn is surrounded by a relief halo or wig. Narrow eyes, a long, thin rectangle of a nose, and a dash of a mouth complete the features which are supported by narrow pointed wings whose feathers are shaped with quarter-moon cuts. The outline of the marker itself is an unusual sloping, two-lobed variety which may have been meant to represent a heart. A simpler version of this type is the Steve Schenek stone, Flatlands Reformed Church, Brooklyn, 1767 (illustrated). Here the carver has returned to a more conventional tympanum and omitted the halo. Two small curlicues in the borders, cut so they seem to lead from the tympanum, provide the only ornamentation. The face is the same basic molded oval pattern as the one on the Antie Schenck stone, but the upturned mouth gives it a happier expression.

Although the identity of the carver of these stones has proved elusive, some evidence survives on the cost of his products. Trinity Church in Manhattan contains several gravestones of the Schenck variety, one of which is the John Bourke stone, 1768. When Bourke's widow listed the various funeral expenses in an inventory of his estate, she listed £4–10–0 "for the setting up of a headstone in the churchyard."[56] Unfortunately, it cannot be determined if this figure also includes charges for physically planting the stone over the grave. Nevertheless, it seems safe to say that the larger percentage of the widow's expenses would have been for the headstone itself. Gravestones of this variety are rare. There are five on Long Island, four in Brooklyn, and one in Queens. Across the East River in Manhattan are eight more. Of the thirteen stones, twelve bear dates from 1764 to 1770. The 1777 date on the Bridget Duggan stone in St. Paul's Chapel churchyard in Manhattan was probably inscribed several years after the symbolic representation itself was carved.

A stone bearing a related design is the Damaris Ludlow stone, Old Prospect Cemetery, Jamaica, 1767 (illustrated). On the evidence of the surrounding stone inscriptions, the name should have read Ludlam. The misspelling was probably the carver's mistake, but for some reason, perhaps lack of choice, the family took it anyway. This diminutive stone bears a rather unusual cherub, wearing closely cropped hair shaped in the Roman fashion. The forehead seems to indent, and below the indentation the face swells into plump, baby-like cheeks. The eyes are shut, slightly slanted, the nose well articulated, and the lips pulled up in a hint of a smile. The overall effect is distinctly oriental. The wings do not seem to go with the face at all, being highly stylized and harkening back to the proto-Zuricher stones.

The carver of the next group of gravestones had one of the longest runs of any of the New York-area stonecutters. His simple but distinctive soul effigies bear dates from 1756 to 1798. Since there are four stones of this type with dates in the 1770's, it seems doubtful that they were all backdated (with the exception of the 1756 stone), hence the determination of a twenty-five-year career seems plausible.

These stones show little individuality, though they vary in height from about a foot and a half to better than four feet, the smaller stones being more common. The effigy itself never varies except in detail. It is an incised or

The Steve Schenek stone, 1767, bears a simple oval without halo.

V

Simple but distinctive soul effigies are found on the Obadiah Mills stone, 1773, and the somewhat more detailed Temmy Brewster stone, 1794.

low-relief face with closed eyes and a rectangular nose whose bottom is formed by a straight line parallel to a tiny straight line of a mouth. Above the face the hair or wig is depicted with a banded ridge. The wings on the effigy spread out and down from the face in a butterfly shape, while the feather directly below the chin is cut like an eyelet.

The Obadiah Mills stone, Old Prospect Cemetery, Jamaica, 1775, (illus. p. 55) is a typical example of this carver's work. Seven stones of this type are located on Long Island in the New York City counties; four of them are inscribed in Dutch. Other stones are in Center Island, Northport, Middle Island and Quogue. Five fine large examples can be found on Strong's Neck. The easternmost stone is in Jamesport. The Northport stone, the Sarah Higbee stone, 1774 (illustrated), differs from the others with its effigy bearing short hair combed forward rather than the banded ridge. On this example one can see how the cutter formed the eyes and nose from one continuous line, a method utilized by several early American gravestone cutters.

The most intriguing of these markers is the Temmy Brewster stone, 1794, Middle Island (illustrated). Not only does it bear a late date for these memorials, but it is a rare example of a slightly different technique. The face is rendered in shallow molded relief and the wings are fashioned delicately with careful detail applied to the feathers. Nevertheless, the shape of the head, the construction of eyes and mouth, and contours of the wings identify the stone as the work of this prolific but anonymous carver.

An interesting, crudely carved variety of stone, which had but little circulation on Long Island, is exemplified by the William Louther stone, St. George's Churchyard, Flushing, 1777 (illustrated). On this sandstone grave marker is carved a round, unpleasant-looking soul effigy with thick, heavy-lidded, closed eyes, a short rectangular nose, and a thick mouth. The entire effigy, including the weak wavy lines meant as feathered wings, is cut on a raised tympanum. According to the inscription, William Loulher was the ensign and adjutant of the Prince of Wales's Royal American Volunteers. He died in February, 1777, five months after the British captured New York and occupied Long Island, which is probably the point at which he joined the Tory regiment of which he was a member. His burial in the burying grounds of an Episcopal church illustrates that denomination's frequent identification with the King's cause during the American Revolution. The only other example of this type of stone on Long Island is the Dutch-language Adrientie Ryder stone, 1776, in the Dutch Reformed Cemetery in Flatbush.

Grace Episcopal Church in Jamaica contains two attractive gravestones which have no mates on the island, or anywhere else in the New York area for that matter. The first, lying flat, south of the path which runs around the east end of the church, is the marker of Richard Betts, 1742 (illustrated). This stone bears a classically derived winged hourglass carved in sharp relief. The lesson of the hourglass is reinforced by the motto, "Tempus Fugit." Along the extreme eastern edge of the churchyard stands the sandstone grave marker of Miriam Hinchman, 1743 (illustrated). On its tympanum, the Archangel Gabriel hovers aloft sounding his horn for the souls of the dead to arise at the hour of the last judgment.

Clockwise from top left, four different unattributed styles: the rudimentary face on the Sarah Higbee stone, 1774, the crudely carved effigy on the William Loulher stone, 1777, the hourglass on the Richard Betts stone, 1742, and the carved Archangel Gabriel on the Miriam Hinchman stone, 1743.

CHAPTER VI

The Revolutionary Period and the
Invasion from the Connecticut Valley

The Revolutionary period forms a watershed in the history of American gravestones. One sign of these turbulent times is the apparent cessation of activity by gravestone carvers who were active in the 1750–1770 period. New styles, cut by different carvers, predominate from the post-Revolutionary period into the beginning of the nineteenth century.

Particularly striking is the rapid decline of the New York-area school of stonecutting. The last Zuricher stone bears a 1778 date, and although Price and his apprentices continued to supply New Jersey burial grounds until the turn of the century, the last stone in his style found on Long Island is dated 1776. Uzal Ward's career on Long Island seems to have ended in 1774. The only exception to this trend is the cutter of the Higbee and Mills type of stones. The decrease in New York-area stones is matched by the lack of advertisements or notices by or about stonecutters in the newspapers of the time. While there were eleven such notices in the 1739–1771 period, there were six between 1777 and 1804.[57]

While there are many gravestones on Long Island bearing dates in the Revolutionary War years, it does seem that they are thin between 1776, the year of the beginning of British occupation, and 1783, when the war came to a close. It is probable that many of these stones were, in fact, cut after the war had ended and backdated. The John Bull stone of Titus and Philetus Conkling, Huntington, 1778, was almost certainly cut later, for not only did the British occupy Huntington, but they used the old burial ground as a campsite. Tradition has it that the British uprooted some of the old stones and made ovens out of them. When bread was baked in these ovens, the epitaphs were reproduced on the loaves, producing a somewhat morbid meal.

Another noticeable difference in Long Island gravestones before and after the Revolution is the scarcity of slate stones in the latter period. To be sure, John Bull and John Stevens III fashioned slate stones in the 1780's which found their way to Long Island—the last dated Stevens stone is dated 1788—but these are exceptions. The almost total disappearance of slate stones after 1780 indicates a change in the trade patterns of Long Islanders away from Massachusetts and Rhode Island, the sources of slate. The last twenty years of the American gravestone-cutting tradition on Long Island saw a great flowering of stones in the graveyards of Suffolk County; most of these stones came from the Connecticut Valley.

The Coastal Style

Connecticut gravestone carvers were among the first to export stones to Long Island. The largest number of eighteenth-century, symbol-engraved markers are their handiwork. Among the several varieties of Connecticut stones reaching Long Island in the 1776–1800 period are a small number of attractively naïve markers bearing incised or low-relief egg-shaped soul effigies hoisted aloft by downward sloping wings. The features are simply drawn with eyes and mouths formed from the same line. Directly behind

The William Stoothoff marker, 1783, is a rare example of a Dutch-language memorial crafted by a New England carver.

The Hannah Helme stone, 1789, cut by Thomas Gold, and the Martha Landon stone, 1775, cut by Michael Baldwin, are similar in their fan-like crowns and downward-sloping wings.

the head a fan-like device suggests a feathered crown. Some of the stones provide a tiny wig for the effigy; others do not.

These markers were cut by Thomas Gold of New Haven (1733–1800). Although the largest number of Gold's Long Island stones are located in Suffolk, he also found customers on the western end of the island and in Manhattan. A Brooklyn example, the Wilhelm Stoothoff marker, 1783, Flatlands (illus. p. 59), is carved in Dutch, the only known instance of a New England carver using that language. Gold's penetration of the New York market was brief; all his Manhattan and western island memorials are dated between 1780 and 1784. Gold's curious appearance in the New York area is traceable to the vicissitudes of the Revolutionary War. Gold belonged to a small religious sect of Scottish origin called the Sandemanians after their founder, Robert Sandeman. The Sandemanians remained loyal to Britain during the Revolution. Several of them, including Gold, fled rebel New Haven for New York in 1778. Gold remained in New York City or its environs until c.1782–84, which is consistent with the dates on his stones found in that area. He then returned to New Haven where he continued to receive commissions for memorials from Long Island families. These later markers are confined to Suffolk.

The shallow-relief versions of Gold's markers are found in Suffolk, most of them in Seaview Cemetery which adjoins Mt. Sinai Congregational Church. One of the better preserved of these memorials is the Hannah Helme marker, 1789, which bears a star in each shoulder finial (illustrated). The latest dated stone of this type is the Mrs. Ruth Brewster stone, 1793, which stands in the Richard "Bull" Smith burial ground in Nissequogue. The Brewster stone is the only one of its type to be carved on slate and is further distinguished by its matching, though simplified, footstone. The most elaborate of all these markers, however, is found further east in Southold. Here can be found the unfortunately disintegrating memorial of Deacon Freegift Wells whose stepped outline and border decoration are clearly related to the Stoothoof marker. The stalk decoration on the borders is very much a Connecticut flourish appearing on Connecticut Valley gravestones from the 1730's.

Another New Haven cutter whose work is similar to Gold's was Michael Baldwin (1719–1787). The magnificently preserved, signed, Martha Landon stone, 1775, Southold (illustrated), shows Baldwin working in a slightly more ambitious style than Gold, though affinities between the two New Haven men are readily perceived. Baldwin's work is rare on Long Island, and the Landon marker may be the only extant example.

The Ornamental Style

From the turn of the seventeenth century onward, the gravestone cutters in the Connecticut Valley were carving stones in a number of characteristic styles. By the mid-1770's they had developed a highly ornamental style which reached Long Island shortly after its introduction by Thomas Johnson I and II of Cromwell.

These stones are extremely ornate, easily among the most ornate stones carved in colonial and federal America. They employ scroll-top arches rather than the simpler triple-lobed format, and the interior borders are carved with complex foliate designs. This style seems to have emerged from a meeting of native Connecticut Valley styles with some of the provincial baroque designs reaching inland from coastal areas.[58] Rather than merely imitating the designs of the provincial baroque derived from engravings, the Johnsons and the Connecticut Valley craftsmen who followed their lead bent these designs to their own stylistic preferences. The result is some of the finest funerary art found on the island.

On Long Island the ornmanetal Connecticut Valley style is largely limited to the North and South Forks with erratic examples showing up in Quogue, East Moriches, and Northport. One of the earliest of these stones on the island, the Mr. Elisha Howell stone, 1777, Quogue (illustrated), shows the style already fully developed. The ornamental Connecticut Valley-style stones are usually quite large, often four to five feet tall. The Howell stone is typical in this respect. It has a double indented scroll tympanum decorated with what appears to be flowers growing out of the acute angle.

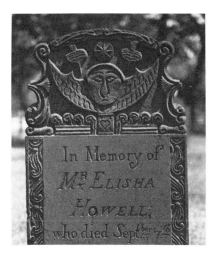

All the Connecticut Valley stones seem to have been divided into two groups: one which attempted stylized portraiture and one which preferred more abstract faces. The carver of the Howell stone preferred the abstract face. Above it is the tiniest of wigs, and at the center is a long bulbous nose. The eyes, teardrop-shaped, tend to be overlarge, and the shape of the mouth suggests that the soul is not entirely happy in its celestial home. The wings are cut in a peculiar indented half-moon pattern reinforcing the image of a soul in heaven. The small symbols above the effigy also appear to be heavenly bodies, though the exact meaning of the large pin-like objects is difficult to surmise. The entire stone is bordered with thick scrollwork.

While the Connecticut Valley ornamental style is noted for ornateness, the Betsey Howell and Catherine Peirson stone, Bridgehampton, 1794 (illustrated), provides a rare example of this style reduced to its basics. The stone is of special interest due to its double image and due to its having been made of marble. The face and general outline of the stone show its clear relationship to the other ornate stones, but its lack of ornamentation, as well as the incised manner of its cutting, sets it apart as unique. Only one other incised version of this style is found on Long Island.

Another version of the ornamental style can be seen on the Thomas Youngs stone, 1793, Greenport (illus. p. 62). The soul effigy is slightly more naturalized than on the other stones. The abstract, half-moon wings of the Elisha Howell stone have given way, here, to something more feathery and realistic. The soul effigy wears an extravagant Crown of Righteousness which resembles a set of pipes for an organ but which is probably meant to be feathers, somewhat along the lines of an Indian war bonnet. Flowers make their appearance on this stone as does the heart, a symbol of the soul's love of Christ, which is appropriately placed under the effigy and above the inscription. Closely related to the Thomas Youngs stone is the Susannah Wiggins stone, 1791, Greenport (illus. p. 62). Here the Crown of Righteousness has given way to a turban-like hairdo, and the tympanum rests on an unusual masonry pattern.

Two versions of the ornamental Connecticut Valley style: the ornate Mr. Elisha Howell stone, 1777, and the simple Betsey Howell and Catherine Peirson stone, 1794.

Some of the Connecticut Valley stonecutters abandoned the abstracted soul effigy for a more naturalistic, molded variety. The Captain Joseph Booth stone, 1795, Greenport (illus. p. 62), shows a full-faced, curly-haired soul effigy whose carefully cut closed eyes suggest eternal sleep.

Belonging to the Connecticut Valley group but not fitting any subcategory very well is the five-foot-tall gravestone of Deacon Josiah Rogers, Northport, 1791 (illus. p. 62). The face of the effigy is clearly related to the

The Thomas Youngs stone, 1793, and the Susannah Wiggins stone, 1791 (left) bear closely-related ornamental images. The Capt. Joseph Booth stone, 1795 (top right) is more naturalistic, while the Josiah Rogers stone, 1791, has elements that hark back to earlier styles.

more abstract style of Connecticut Valley soul effigies though somewhat more polished and wearing a wig that is a throwback to the styles of the mid-eighteenth century. The wings are also atypical for this kind of stone.

Closely related to the Connecticut Valley ornamental style are those cut by the Manning family of eastern Connecticut. Their stones, unlike the sandstone markers from the Connecticut Valley, are cut in granite, and are generally plainer, without the detail and ornamentation of the Connecticut Valley ornamental stone. The faces on the Manning soul effigies, such as the Abigail Hand stone, 1791, Sagaponack (illustrated), bear grotesque features and goggle-eyes, a technique which also shapes the downturned mouth. The effigy's hair, or Crown of Righteousness, starts wildly from the head, reinforcing the generally savage appearance of the stone. All the secondary motifs tend to be of a simple scroll motif, while the wings display no detailing whatever. The Daniel Moore stone, 1791, Bridgehampton (illustrated), is an example of the Manning style cut on a "cradle back" stone. Several members of this family cut stones in similar styles. The Hand stone shows similarities with those carved by Rockwell Manning, while the Moore stone bears greater resemblance to Frederick's work. On Long Island, Manning stones are far less common than Connecticut Valley stones and are limited to seven examples on the East End.

The Common Style Post-Revolutionary Stone

In addition to the ornamental Connecticut Valley stones and their relatives from the eastern part of Connecticut, other gravestones of less ornate design were imported across the Sound and erected in the burial grounds of Long Island, particularly in Suffolk County. One of these stones, the Samuel Jagger stone, 1785, Mattituck, with its Indian-like symbol, does not fit easily in any category. There were, however, two varieties of a single style cut in such numbers and so widely distributed that they deserve to be called the common post-revolutionary style. These stones, found from the two Forks and Gardiner's Island to as far west as Oyster Bay, appear to be descended from the flared-wing variety of the 1740's. After a period of thirty years or so the flared-wing variety evolved into a more attenuated and less floral version. Some of these stones bear dates as early as the 1760's, but it is likely that these are replacement stones. The greatest number in this style bear dates from the 1780's and 1790's. Like the other symbol-carved stones, they barely outlasted the turn of the century; the latest date found is 1807. The basic soul effigy design for these stones was aparently developed by Peter Buckland of Hartford County. However, other cutters such as Charles Dolph, Isaac Sweetland, craftsmen in the Middletown area and the Hill family made them as well.

In appearance these stones are very much alike, usually two to three feet in height, cut in a rather low-grade brown sandstone (except for two odd slates found in the churchyard of the Whaler's Church in Sag Harbor). Many are disintegrating while much older stones near them are in excellent condition. The only real difference found in these stones, a difference which mirrors that in the ornamental style, is that one group utilizes an inverted teardrop soul effigy while the other version utilizes a more naturalistic representation. The Jane Osborn stone, 1802, East Hampton (illus. p. 64), exemplifies the first, and the Sally Halsey stone, 1804, Sag Harbor (illus. p. 64), is a superlative representation of the second. Otherwise the

Stones cut by the Manning family: the Abigail Hand stone and the Daniel Moore stone, both 1791, exhibit the family's idiosyncratic soul effigies.

The two patterns of the common post-revolutionary styles are illustratedby the inverted tear-drop soul effigy on the Jane Osborn stone, 1802, and the naturalistic image on the Sally Halsey stone, 1801.

wings with their short slash-like quarter moons and dashes and the broad stylized feather Crowns of Righteousness are cut from the same mold. Subsidiary designs, when found at all, are limited to narrow scroll or line work on the borders. Frequently the footstone is carved with a fleur-de-lis. This was apparently used by several carvers, and thus cannot be considered a Buckland workshop mark.

It was not lack of ability which led Buckland and his imitators to carve the same essential design in such huge quantities. Buckland himself fashioned several gravestones carved in the ornamental design. Exeptional versions of the Connecticut Valley stock pattern can be found as well. They demonstrate that Buckland, Dolph, and the other Connecticut Valley carvers who followed their lead were capable of producing more individualized patterns even on their cheaper stones. The question is, why did they not?

It may be that, like Henry Ford and the Model T, Connecticut Valley craftsmen designed their stones for general appeal, priced them within the range of nearly every family, and, when it proved popular, gave over almost their entire production to this one pattern until it flooded their market area. The careers of these stone carvers are another episode in the ancient struggle between commercial success and artistic achievement. Other stonecutters, notably the second two John Stevenses, experienced a similar conflict, but neither surrendered so completely to the lure of the marketplace. In doing so, however, Buckland and his colleagues must have been following or anticipating the tone of the times. Unless the populace of New England and Long Island was willing to accept such a monotony of design, they would never have achieved such apparent success. Once again the popularity, or lack of it, of gravestone designs seems to reflect a shift in religious attitudes among the people the gravestone cutters served. It is hard to doubt that these markers were churned out to meet the demands of a market which had largely ceased to expect imagination or quality, a market which bought stones with religious symbolism out of convention rather than conviction. It should be no surprise, then, that Buckland and his fellow craftsmen bring down the curtain on the native gravestone-cutting tradition.

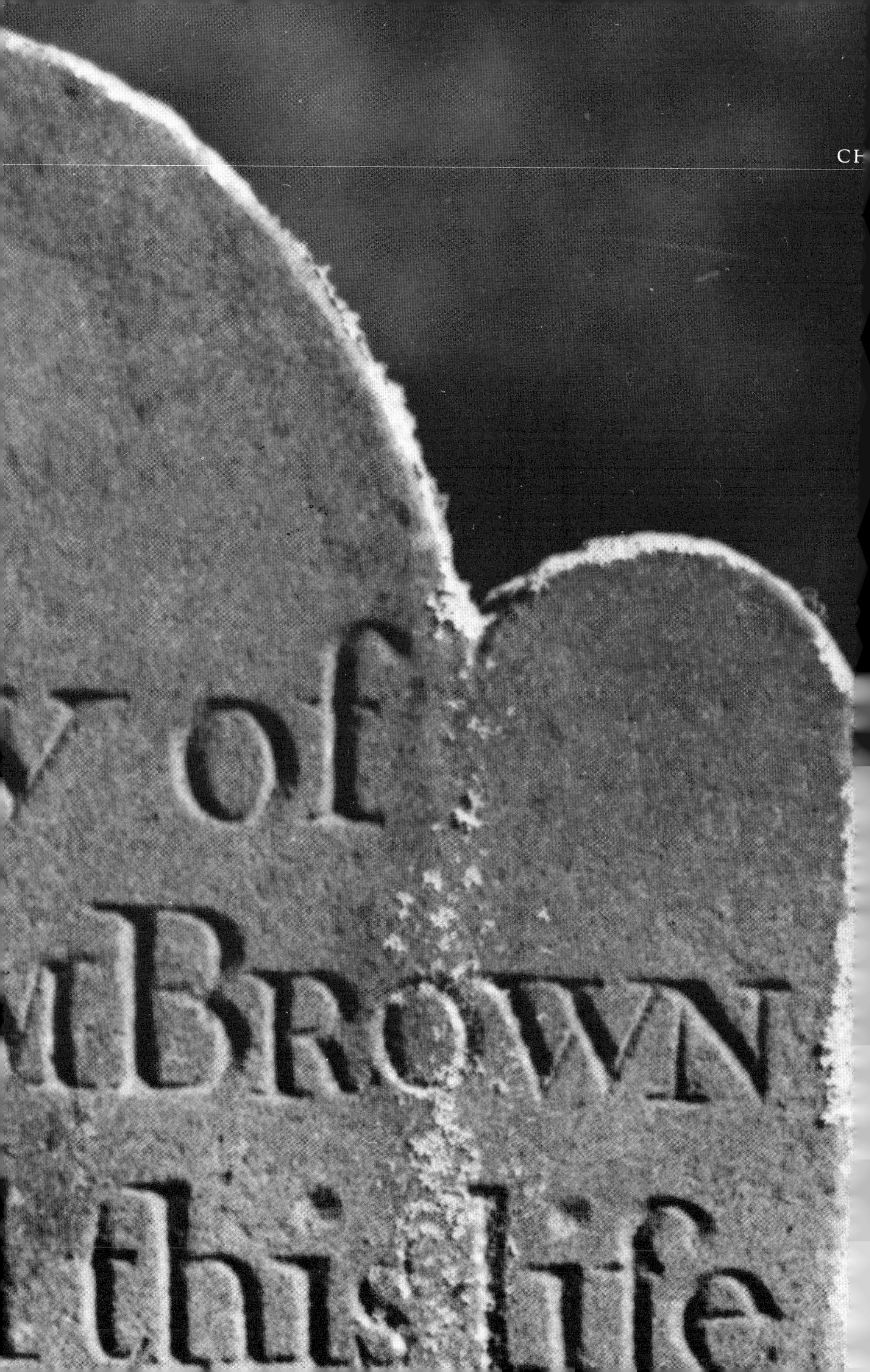
y of
BROWN
this life

The End of the Tradition, 1790–1810

The American gravestone-cutting tradition which began in the mid-seventeenth century and flourished through the eighteenth century died most suddenly around the year 1800. Soul effigy stones were carved right up to the year of 1800. They then almost entirely ceased to exist. After that date there are relatively few stones appearing with the old symbolic representations. Most of these, the last of which is dated 1807, are of the common post-revolutionary style. Little of the traditional iconography was carved thereafter.

The demise of the tradition of cutting native funerary symbols on gravestones is usually laid to the adoption of the neo-classical styles coming into the new republic. Some researchers go so far as to say these styles were deliberately chosen in order to give the United States an artistic style imbued with a classical republican spirit, hence the stylistic craze for Greek and Roman motifs. This argument begs the question of why this style was also popular in European monarchies (most of these classical patterns were coming into the United States from fiercely monarchical Great Britain). The truth is that the late eighteenth century was the time of a great neo-classical revival which had little to do with the nature of the governments of the countries involved. The most prevalent of the neo-classical funerary styles were the urn, willow, or urn and willow combined, expressions of loss both secularized and sentimentalized which were found not only on gravestones but on embroidered and printed mourning pieces as well. The effect on the artistic appearance of American cemeteries was immense. As Alan Ludwig puts it, "By 1800 almost every burial ground in New England, save for those sunk in a total rural atmosphere, reflected the forms and themes of the new style."[59]

While this is generally true in New England, it is not precisely what happened on Long Island. True, the old religious symbols did fall into disuse around the turn of the nineteenth century, but they were not instantly replaced by the neo-classical motifs. While the urn and willow designs did make their appearance on Long Island with the demise of the traditional symbols, they never took over the burial grounds as completely as they did in New England. There are no Long Island counterparts to the long rows of tall, nearly identical, slate urn and willow stones such as are found in the cemeteries around Boston. In fact, neo-classical designs are not common on Long Island during the transitional period from 1790 to 1810. The earliest example of this style on Long Island is the Charles Smith stone, East Moriches, 1793 (illustrated), probably cut in New Jersey, which sports a delicate monogram over the symbol at the top. A good example of the urn carved in relief is the Betsy Byram stone, 1797, North Haven (illustrated).

The truth of the matter is that there was a lag on Long Island between the time the old styles died out and the new ones gained wide circulation. The urn and willow seem to have enjoyed their greatest popularity on Long Island between 1820 and 1850 when they were cut on white marble supplied from Vermont (illus. p. 69). By this time, however, even the urn and willow were slowly giving way to the plain white marble rectangles that reigned supreme over nineteenth-century American burial grounds until they were supplanted towards the end of the nineteenth century by

Urns appear on the tympanums of the Charles Smith stone, 1793, and the Betsy Byram stone, 1797. Opposite: the Capt. Gersham Brown stone, an example of a late eighteenth-century unadorned memorial.

the most undistinguished of all funerary monuments — the still-favored granite slab.

The type of stone which did achieve great popularity in the wake of the religious-symboled stones and before the neo-classical styles really caught on was the plain, three-lobed sandstone variety simply inscribed "In Memory" or "In Memorium" with the deceased's name, birth and death dates, and sometimes an epitaph inscribed below. These stones, apparently carved by the Hills as well as in New York–New Jersey and Connecticut, are common all over the island (illus. p. 66).

The urn-and-willow design was a step backward in gravestone art for several reasons. To begin with, these images generally lack the visual interest and impact of the traditionally engraved stones. The very nature of the symbols was far more limiting than the earlier symbols of death and resurrection which lent themselves to a great variety of beautiful, striking, and sometimes awesome designs. Spiritual symbols represented the mysteries of time and eternity rather than the bland sentimentality of the newer styles. Lastly, the earlier stones sprang from an American consciousness and were developed in a specifically American milieu. They became, in fact, the symbol of faith of a large segment of the American people. The new symbols, imported entirely from abroad, represented European popular taste.

This leaves us with the final question: Why did Americans turn their backs on their native funerary imagery and accept the neo-classical designs? Some commentators have seen this as an early manifestation of American feelings of cultural inferiority towards everything European. Such impulses were at work, but they fail as a complete explanation. Perhaps, on Long Island, the collapse of traditional gravestone art was not quite as sudden as it might first appear. Consider the vogue for the common post-revolutionary gravestone, a type of marker churned out in great numbers bearing nearly identical designs. These stones seem to point to a commercialization and decadence in the craft of gravestone-cutting itself.

The disappearance of the old funerary symbols resulted from great social changes encompassing a deterioration of the early religious spirit. On Long Island this fact is supported by the fading of religious symbolism first on the western parts of the island. The western parts of Long Island contained a more heterogeneous population than the eastern areas. Puritan churches near New York City had to compete with strong Anglican, Quaker, Lutheran, and Dutch Reformed churches. Piety was never strongly entrenched in city-dominated areas which were already noted for the materialism of their society by the mid-eighteenth century. In New York City, New Jersey, and western Long Island, the Puritan example in developing medieval funerary symbols was followed only so long as it was compatible with the religious outlook of the largely non-Puritan population. Any general softening of religious belief would be felt in those sections which lay within New York City's increasingly powerful cultural influence. When this occurred, the gravestone symbolism which had expressed earlier attitudes and beliefs was abandoned.

The east end of the island, more religiously and socially homogenous and with strong traditional ties to New England, held on at least to the external forms of Puritanism for another twenty years. By this time, however, even in New England, the Puritan motherland, the old funerary symbols were dying out, and continental and urban influences were penetrating Suffolk from Manhattan.[60]

Puritanism died out around the turn of the eighteenth century. If the earlier religious doctrines appeared anachronistic to more and more people, then the symbols which represented those beliefs must have had less and less meaning. With this in mind, the inability of the old symbols to compete with the fashionable new motifs coming in from Europe becomes understandable.

Willows cut in white marble dominate the James Carll stone, 1845, and the Ann Stewart stone, 1819.

The Hill Family

Among the most attractive of Long Island's gravestones are those carved by Ithuel Hill, the only documented resident cutter of the 1680–1800 period. Hill descended from an old Connecticut family which originated in the Farmington-Harwinton area but later moved to Norwalk. Ithuel emigrated to Sag Harbor shortly after marrying Isabel Cornwall in 1789. Both his grandfather and father had been stonecutters, and Ithuel followed the family tradition, quite possibly selling his stones to Long Island families even before his emigration. Though Hill's carving, especially his soul effigies, shows the influence of Connecticut Valley carvers, his style exhibits a great deal of individuality, particularly on his portrait markers which were his most distinctive product. Hill also set himself off from his contemporaries by being among the first to use marble as his medium of choice. Marble was rare on Long Island before 1820, and most stones of that type before that date seem to be his work.

Hill and his assistants carved soul effigies (illustrated), portrait stones (illus. p. 72), neo-classical designs (illus. p. 72), and masonic emblems. They are typically carved in delicate low relief. For his portrait markers Hill favored a three-quarter view, especially for men's stones. The female portrait (illus. p. 72), usually full-faced and less elaborate than the male, was the only pattern Hill repeated, the others varying in some respect. Most of Hill's portraits are set off by lace or ruffles.

Occasionally, Hill crafted a monument which featured several types of symbols. The Hainulal Horton marker, 1809, Sag Harbor (illus. p. 72), features a portrait as its central symbol, but this is flanked by two neo-classical columns, while an angel hovers in the upper reaches of the tympanum.

In addition to the "I Hill sculpt" which he sometimes engraved at the bottom of his stones, several characteristic flourishes identify Hill markers. Regardless of the symbol, most of his designs incorporate a device resembling a parenthesis with a bulge at either end ⟨⟩. Hill used this configuration to form ruffles, column finials, clouds, flowers, and more abstract decorations. Another favored touch was an ornate, usually downward spiralling, curlicue placed just beneath the inscription.

Written evidence supports the belief that the spiralling curlicue was originally a Hill workshop mark. On July 5, 1814, Hill, then working in Huntington, sent Mrs. Nancy Davids of Southold his bill for "a good and hansom pare of white marble Grave Stones" which he had carved for her husband, Samuel, who had died December 23, 1811.[61] The stone is a large, plain white marble marker, unexceptional but for the lengthy epitaph recounting Davids' death in a shipwreck during a sudden winter storm on the sound. In addition to the lithe Roman letters favored by Hill, the stone features the distinctive curlicue just below the epitaph. Another design apparently favored by the Hill family, a broken sunburst ◁ ⫯ ▷, separates the inscription from the epitaph. Hill's fee, collected at Southold by his son, John C. Hill, was $40 plus $3.50 for shipping the stones to the Smith Family burial ground in Nissequogue where Davids was buried. Interestingly, the bill is rendered in both United States dollars and in the old English

Opposite: Ithuel Hill's style of soul effigy is well represented by the Nancy Landon stone, 1801.

The Luther Storrs stone, 1804, illustrates Hill's distinctive portrait pattern; the Joshua Benjamin stone, 1804, boasts one of his neo-classical urn designs.

The Abigail Gardiner stone, 1800, bears Hill's usual stylized female portrait, while the Hainulal Horton stone, 1809, mingles portrait and neo-classical symbols.

monetary system, the latter being calculated at £17–6–0.[62]. Mrs. Davids paid in United States currency.

Ithuel Hill was aided in gravestone carving by his son John C. and possibly by his other son Samuel. He was briefly joined by his brother Phineas, who emigrated with him to Sag Harbor but returned to Connecticut after a year. Two free males under sixteen are listed in Ithuel's household at Sag Harbor in 1790. One of these was probably John C.; the other most likely Phineas.[63] In 1820 when Ithuel was back in Sag Harbor, perhaps after a stay in Huntington, Hill's household included a boy under sixteen and another male between sixteen and twenty-six. Two persons, Ithuel and the older male, are described as being engaged in manufacture.[64].

Ithuel Hill seemed plagued by ill health and died on a recuperative visit to Martha's Vineyard in 1821. His family, however, is unique, for it has continued in the gravestone-carving business down to the present day. Phineas Hill (1778–1844) returned to Connecticut after a brief stay with his brother Ithuel but came back to Long Island in 1821, this time to Huntington. In 1839 he moved to Hempstead where he produced gravestones. In 1843, he moved to Riverhead where he died in 1844. Though the immediate descendants of Ithuel died out, Phineas's line survives, and the George Hill Moore Monument Company in Riverhead is descended from him. By the time of Ithuel's death, however, the old traditional symbolism had died out, and the later Hills produced mostly urn and willow markers and plain stones. Today, standard sand-blasted granite memorials are made.

Forty-two of Ithuel Hill's symbol-carved stones still stand on Long Island, mostly on the East End. They bear dates from 1792 to 1817. Hill's plain markers are spread throughout Suffolk County.

The Burial Grounds of Long Island

The physical condition of early Long Island burial grounds varies greatly. Some are derelict, abandoned by the churches, families, and communities which established and used them, and occasionally so preyed upon by vandals that even their basic identity as burial grounds is obscured or obliterated. At the opposite end of the spectrum are those burial grounds which are among the jewels of Long Island antiquities, wonderfully cared for and preserved, located in picturesque settings. Most of Long Island's colonial and federal burial grounds lie somewhere between the two extremes mentioned above. The city counties have suffered the worst, as far as the destruction of early burial grounds is concerned. Many were simply blotted out of existence as the forces of urban expansion gained momentum earlier in this century, and some burial grounds in New York City lay unseen, and sometimes unknown, beneath playgrounds, apartment houses, and streets. Fortunately, most of the surviving burial grounds in Brooklyn or Queens are now under the protection of one type of agency or another, and chances for survival are generally good.

One of the more remarkable things about the gravestones of the 1680–1810 period is not that so many show signs of age, deterioration, or abuse, but rather that so many are in good, fine, and occasionally mint condition. Gravestones are subject to deterioration and destruction from a number of sources. Moss and lichens can mar and possibly weaken the rock structure. Water permeates the stone and, upon freezing, expands, creating fissures which usually result in pieces of the stone shaling off. This is especially noticable in a porous material such as sandstone. The ordinary effects of weather, climate, and atmosphere will slowly wear down any stone, though it may take centuries for them to have any serious effect, and those gravestones subject to sea breeze seem to wear more quickly than those in more sheltered areas. Air pollution also hastens the deterioration of stones. Researchers at the Brookhaven National Laboratory at Upton, Long Island, have developed chemical compounds which can preserve stones for great periods of time, though only removal to a protected environment will do so indefinitely.

While natural forces take their toll of the early gravestones, the greatest threat to their existence, and that of the burial grounds which hold them, comes from human sources. Man-made destruction comes from vandalism, which appears to be the special province of adolescents responding to some demonic instinct to destroy, and from more conscious and purposeful, if unjustified, destruction, as in the callous obliteration of a burial ground in the course of building subdivisions or cutting roads. The problem of vandalism seems to be on the increase, and it probably owes something to the breakdown of community traditions and spirit which has accompanied the enormous growth of Long Island since 1945. Nevertheless, there are recorded instances of gravestones being taken from burial grounds and used as the foundations of barns and as walkways dating from the nineteenth century. In 1936 the citizens of Miller Place, then presumably descended largely from early Long Island settler stock, complacently and approvingly allowed the Miller burial ground, containing the grave of the village's eponymous founder, to be bulldozed during the construction of a school. Such destruction also occurred on the rural and history-conscious East End. In June, 1947, Harry B. Squires of Bridgehampton wrote the editor of the *Long Island Forum:* "New highways have been built over some of these groups of ancient graves and in one case a swimming pool now stands over the graves of some of our early settlers."[65]

Several towns and municipalities are taking measures to preserve their colonial and federal burial grounds. East Hampton and Southampton provide regular maintenance of their early burial grounds, although town workers should be told not to strike the gravestones with their power lawnmowers when cutting the grass. Scratches and scrapes are noticeable on many gravestones on the South Fork and some have been permanently damaged. The North Fork villages are equally diligent and the East End burial grounds are among the best preserved on the island. This is partly attributable to a sense of community and traditions, though much is probably due to the low population density, particularly after the summer season. Protection and maintenance from the other Long Island towns is more spasmodic and depends on the concern and interest exerted by the citizenry. The Town of Huntington, which has several fine burial grounds that date from the 1680–1810 period, also has a serious vandalism problem. In response, the town approved an ordinance prohibiting entrance to the town's burial grounds between sunset and sunrise. Enforcement of a law is the key to its success, and even though Rufus Langhans, the current town historian, has expressed his willingness to prosecute those disturbing the town's burial grounds if given information by the citizens, no information has been forthcoming, and the destruction goes on.

Another increasingly ominous problem is that of gravestone theft. Gravestone theft appears to be a negative side effect of the growing appreciation and interest in early American gravestone art. "Reputable" antique dealers in New York City have already expressed their willingness to handle any of the colonial or federal gravestones supplied them, although such trade is clearly illegal. Between the vandals and the thieves, not to mention the inexorable pressures of time and weather, it is becoming more and more inevitable that the best of the surviving gravestones will have to be removed to protected areas to ensure their continued existence. This has already been done in a limited number of instances in New England but, to date, only Huntington has taken such action on Long Island.

All Long Island's colonial and federal burial grounds can benefit from additional interest and protection. Many are in need of restoration, and most require additional maintenance. Historical societies and local members of the Association for Gravestone Studies should be listing and photographing all Long Island's surviving gravestones, making special note of those which should be removed for permanent safekeeping. Legal measures should then be undertaken to effect such removal. Archeological investigations should also be made of the 1680–1810 burial grounds. The large number of surviving gravestones which stand or lie half sunken in the ground suggests many more may lie beneath the surface. What such stones might add to our knowledge of the typology and use of gravestones on Long Island is difficult to predict, but certainly such investigations must be considered promising.

The following is a list of gravestone carvers whose work is found on Long Island. An asterisk indicates carvers whose work on the island is probable, but not definite.

I. New York-New Jersey

Thomas Brown (fl. 1764–1794)
William Grant, New York City (fl. 1740–1770)
Ithuel Hill, Sag Harbor (died 1821)
John C. Hill, Sag Harbor (fl. 1820)
Phineas Hill, Sag Harbor (1778–1844)
Ebenezar Price, Elizabeth, New Jersey (1728–1788)
_____ Turner (?) (fl. 1730)
Uzal Ward, Newark, New Jersey (fl. 1750–1787)
John Zuricher, New York City (and Rockland)
    (fl. 1740–1784)

The following men advertised themselves as gravestone carvers in eighteenth century New York City newspapers. While they have yet to be connected with a particular gravestone style, they are likely to prove responsible for several types of stone still unattributable. Dates are those of their advertisements.

Charles Bromfield (1770)
Anthony Dodane (1768, 1769)
Robert Hartley (1771)

II. Connecticut

Michael Baldwin, New Haven (1719–1787)
Peter Barker, Montville (fl. 1750)*
Peter Buckland, East Hartford (1738–1816)
William Buckland, Jr., East Hartford (1727–1795)
Benjamin Collins, Lebanon (1691–1759)
Charles Dolph, Saybrook (1776–1815)*
Thomas Gold (1733–1800)
John Hartshorn, Norwich (fl. c.1720)
Joseph Johnson, Middletown (1698–?)
Thomas Johnson, Middletown (1690–1761)
Thomas Johnson, Middletown/Cromwell (1718–1774)
Thomas Johnson, Middletown (1750–1789)
Frederick Manning, Windham (1758–1806)
Josiah Manning, Windham (1760–1806)
Rockwell Manning, Norwich (1760–1806)
Isaac Sweetland, Hartford (fl. 1789)*
James Stanclift, Portland (1634–1712)
James Stanclift, Portland (1692–1772)
James Stanclift, Portland (1712–1785)*

III. Massachusetts

Abraham Codner, Boston (died 1750)*
William Codner, Boston (1709–1769)
Henry Emmes, Boston (fl. 1750)
Nathaniel Emmes, Boston (1690–1750)*
James Foster, Dorchester (1732–1771)*
Nathaniel Fuller, Plympton (1687–1758)
Henry Christian Geyer, Boston (fl. 1775)
John Homer, Boston (1727–c.1803)
Caleb Lamson, Charlestown (1697–1767)
John Lamson, Charlestown (1732–1778)*
Joseph Lamson, Charlestown (1731–1789)*
Nathaniel Lamson, Charlestown (1693–1755)
William Mumford, Boston (1641–1718)
Thomas Welch, Charlestown (1655–1763)*

IV. Rhode Island

John Anthony Angell, Providence (d. 1756)*
John Bull, Newport (1734–1808)
John Stevens, Newport (1646–1736)
John Stevens, Newport (1702–1778)
John Stevens, Newport (fl. 1770–1789)
William Stevens, Newport (1710–1794)*
Phillip Stevens, Newport (1793–1866)*
Henry Bull (fl. 1788)

APPENDIX II

The following charts list those 1680–1810 burial grounds which are not thoroughly destroyed and whose stones date from the period under discussion rather than being back-dated replacement markers. Miscellaneous refers to fieldstone markers, symbols which do not fit any of the other categories, and late eighteenth century "In Memory" stones.

	Early Massachusetts 1620–1720	Lamson Workshop/Rounded Skull	Misc. Massachusetts	Stevens Workshop/John Bull	Early Connecticut Valley 1680–1730	Connecticut Valley Flared-Ear 1730–1770
1. *New Utrecht Dutch Reformed Churchyard* New Utrecht, Brooklyn						
2. *Gravesend-Van Sicklen Cemetery* Gravesend, Brooklyn						
3. *Dutch Reformed Churchyard* Flatbush, Brooklyn						
4. *Dutch Reformed Churchyard* Flatlands, Brooklyn						
5. *Alsop Burial Ground* Long Island City, Queens						
6. *Lawrence Manor Burying Ground* Steinway, Queens						
7. *Riker Cemetery* Astoria, Queens						
8. *St. Georges Churchyard* Flushing, Queens						
9. *Grace Episcopal Churchyard* Jamaica, Queens				🌀		
10. *Old Prospect Cemetery* Jamaica, Queens						🌀
11. *Old Springfield Cemetery* Springfield Gardens, Queens						
12. *Hewlett Burial Plot* Great Neck						
13. *St. Georges Churchyard* Hempstead, Nassau						
14. *Woolsey Burial Ground* Glen Cove		🌀	🌀			🌀
15. *McLoughlin-Street Burial Ground* Glen Cove						
16. *Frost Burial Ground* Lattingtown						
17. *Smith-Ludlam Cemetery* Center Island		🌀				
18. *Tilley Burial Ground* Mill Neck						
19. *Townsend-Mill Pond Burial Ground* Oyster Bay		🌀		🌀		
20. *Townsend-Wortman Burial Ground* Mill River Road, Oyster Bay		🌀				
21. *Old Baptist Churchyard* Oyster Bay		🌀				
22. *Fortified Hill Burial Ground* Oyster Bay				🌀		

Connecticut Valley Ornamental Style/Manning Family	Buckland Workshop	Misc. Connecticut	New York–New Jersey Death's Heads	Zuricher Workshop	Uzal Ward/William Grant	Misc. New York–New Jersey	Hill Family	Urn & Willow	Misc.
						✿		✿	✿
				✿		✿			
				✿		✿		✿	
				✿		✿		✿	
			✿	✿					✿
			✿	✿		✿			✿
						✿			✿
						✿			
			✿	✿		✿			✿
			✿			✿			✿
			✿	✿		✿		✿	✿
				✿		✿			
	✿	✿				✿			✿
	✿								✿
									✿
		✿							✿
						✿			✿
									✿
						✿			✿
	✿		✿						✿
				✿		✿			✿
		✿		✿					

Connecticut Valley Ornamental Style/Manning Family	Buckland Workshop	Misc. Connecticut	New York–New Jersey Death's Heads	Zuricher Workshop	Uzal Ward/William Grant	Misc. New York–New Jersey	Hill Family	Urn & Willow	Misc.
		✹				✹			✹
		✹							
									✹
								✹	
	✹								✹
				✹					
		✹		✹					✹
	✹							✹	
								✹	
	✹	✹		✹				✹	✹
							✹		
	✹	✹		✹					
	✹						✹		✹
✹									
	✹								
	✹							✹	
		✹					✹		
								✹	
	✹		✹			✹			✹
		✹							✹
			✹	✹	✹	✹	✹		✹
	✹						✹		✹
	✹								
	✹	✹					✹	✹	✹

	Early Massachusetts 1620–1720	Lamson Workshop/Rounded Skull	Misc. Massachusetts	Stevens Workshop/John Bull	Early Connecticut Valley 1680–1730	Connecticut Valley Flared-Ear 1730–1770
47. *Caroline Episcopal Church* Setauket		✳				
48. *Hawkins-Smith Burial Ground* South Setauket						
49. *Smith-Strong Burial Ground* Strong's Neck						
50. *Seaview Burial Ground* Mt. Sinai						
51. *Overton-Smith Burial Ground* Coram						
52. *Still Burial Ground* Coram						
53. *Hawkins Burial Ground* Yaphank			✳			
54. *Havens-Young Burial Ground* Center Moriches						
55. *Josiah Smith Burial Ground* East Moriches			✳	✳		
56. *Hallock Burial Ground* Rocky Point						
57. *Wading River Burial Ground* Wading River						
58. *Westhampton Burial Ground* Westhampton				✳		
59. *Quogue Burial Ground* Quogue				✳		
60. *North End Burial Ground* Southampton		✳	✳	✳	✳	
61. *South End Burial Ground* Southampton	✳	✳			✳	✳
62. *Public Cemetery* Southampton		✳		✳	✳	
63. *Flying Point Burial Ground* Southampton		✳		✳	✳	
64. *Water Mill Burial Ground* Water Mill	✳	✳		✳		
65. *Newlight Lane Burial Ground* Bridgehampton		✳				✳
66. *Bridgehampton Presbyterian Churchyard* Bridgehampton				✳		
67. *Evergreen Cemetery* Bridgehampton						✳
68. *Mecox Burial Ground* Mecox	✳	✳			✳	✳
69. *Sagaponack Burial Ground* Sagponack	✳		✳	✳	✳	✳
70. *Wainscott Burial Ground* Wainscott						

Connecticut Valley Ornamental Style/Manning Family	Buckland Workshop	Misc. Connecticut	New York–New Jersey Death's Heads	Zuricher Workshop	Uzal Ward/William Grant	Misc. New York–New Jersey	Hill Family	Urn & Willow	Misc.
							✲	✲	
	✲								
		✲				✲			✲
	✲	✲							
	✲					✲			✲
	✲								✲
								✲	
	✲								
✲	✲							✲	
✲	✲							✲	
	✲								✲
						✲			
✲	✲				✲	✲			
✲	✲	✲	✲	✲	✲	✲			✲
✲		✲				✲			✲
							✲		
✲									
	✲								
✲		✲							
✲	✲	✲							✲
✲							✲		
	✲	✲							
✲	✲		✲						
		✲				✲			✲

	Early Massachusetts 1620–1720	Lamson Workshop/Rounded Skull	Misc. Massachusetts	Stevens Workshop/John Bull	Early Connecticut Valley 1680–1730	Connecticut Valley Flared-Ear 1730–1770
71. *Georgica Burial Ground* Georgica						
72. *South End Burial Ground* East Hampton	✺	✺		✺	✺	✺
73. *North End Burial Ground* East Hampton				✺		
74. *Amagansett Burial Ground* Amagansett		✺		✺		
75. *Parsons Burial Ground* Springs				✺		
76. *First House Burial Ground* Montauk				✺		
77. *Prebyterian "Whalers" Churchyard* Sag Harbor						
78. *Edwards Burial Ground* Sag Harbor				✺		
79. *Payne-Byrams Burial Ground* North Haven						
80. *Presbyterian Churchyard* Shelter Island		✺		✺		
81. *Baiting Hollow Burial Ground* Baiting Hollow				✺		
82. *Riverhead Cemetery* Riverhead				✺		
83. *Aquebogue Burial Ground* Aquebogue				✺		
84. *Jamesport Burial Ground* Jamesport		✺		✺		✺
85. *Mattituck Presbyterian Churchyard* Mattituck		✺		✺	✺	✺
86. *Cutchogue Burial Ground* Cutchogue	✺			✺		✺
87. *Presbyterian Churchyard* Southold	✺	✺	✺	✺	✺	✺
88. *Conkling Burial Ground* Southold		✺		✺		
89. *Stirling Cemetery* Greenport		✺		✺		
90. *Terry Burial Ground* Orient						
91. *Beebee Burial Ground* Orient						
92. *Brown's Hill Burial Ground* Orient	✺	✺		✺	✺	
93. *Village Burial Ground* Orient						

Connecticut Valley Ornamental Style/Manning Family	Buckland Workshop	Misc. Connecticut	New York–New Jersey Death's Heads	Zuricher Workshop	Uzal Ward/William Grant	Misc. New York–New Jersey	Hill Family	Urn & Willow	Misc.
✷									
✷	✷	✷					✷	✷	✷
	✷					✷		✷	✷
	✷								
									✷
✷	✷	✷					✷	✷	
✷	✷							✷	
	✷					✷		✷	
	✷								
✷	✷								
	✷				✷				
✷	✷	✷		✷	✷				
✷	✷							✷	
✷	✷	✷		✷				✷	
✷	✷	✷		✷			✷	✷	✷
✷	✷	✷						✷	
	✷								
	✷								
	✷						✷	✷	

FOOTNOTES

1. Alan I. Ludwig, *Graven Images* (Middletown, Connecticut: Wesleyan University Press, 1968), 274.

2. A full discussion of the English gravestone-cutting tradition and its possible links with American developments is found in Ludwig, *ibid.*, 239–274.

3. Benjamin Thompson, *History of Long Island*, II (New York, 1843), 92.

4. Robert Payne, *The Island* (New York: Harcourt, Brace & Co., 1959), 237–238.

5. In addition to the English examples cited by Ludwig see Brian DeBreffney and George Mott, *The Churches and Abbeys of Ireland* (New York: W. W. Norton and Co., 1970), 120, and Betty Willsher and Doreen Hunter, *Stones: 18th Century Scottish Gravestones* (New York: Taplinger Publishing Co., 1979).

6. James Bertram, *Brasses and Brass Rubbing in England* (New York: Great Albion Books, 1971), 55–56.

7. The striking exceptions to this generalization are a number of gravestones carved in the Medway Valley of Kent, England, between 1670 and 1770. These stones, the work of the "Maidstone Carvers," bear certain resemblances to the work of New England gravestone carvers, particularly those of rural areas. The Medway Valley was known for its Puritan and nonconformist sympathies in the seventeenth and eighteenth centuries. A large number of the early colonists of Massachusetts Bay, many of whom subsequently migrated to eastern Long Island, came from the Medway Valley. It should be noted, however, that the Medway stones appeared at a time when the New England tradition was already established, and though there are obvious similarities between the two groups, there are also noticeable differences. Further research may demonstrate a closer relationship between the Medway and American gravestones, but at present the resemblances between them seem best explained by the similar pattern of development experienced by the societies in which they appeared. See Peter Benes, *The Masks of Orthodoxy, Folk Gravestone Carving in Plymouth County, Massachusetts, 1689–1805* (Amherst, Massachusetts: University of Massachusetts Press, 1977), 185–190.

8. David E. Stannard, *The Puritan Way of Death* (New York: Oxford University Press, 1977), 108.

9. Letter of Lord Cornbury to the Board of Trade, June 30, 1703, from E. B. O'Callaghan (ed.), *The Documentary History of the State of New York*, I, 1058, cited in Dean Failey, *Long Island is My Nation: The Decorative Arts and Craftsmen, 1640–1830* (Setauket, New York: Society for the Preservation of Long Island Antiquities, 1976), 13.

10. *Ibid.*

11. "The Humble Address of the Governor and Council of Your Majesty's Province of New York," O'Callaghan, 208, cited in Failey, 13.

12. John Lion Gardiner, "Gardiner's East Hampton," *Collections of the New-York Historical Society* (New York: Printed for the Society, 1869), 271, cited in Failey, 5.

13. Stannard, 112.

14. Reverend Ebenezer Prime, *A Sermon Preached in Oyster Bay, February 27, 1743/4, at the Funeral of Mrs. Freelove Wilmot* (New York: James, Parker, 1744).

15. Gabriel Furman, *Antiquities of Long Island* (J. W. Bouton, 1874, reprint Port Washington, New York: Ira J. Friedman, 1971), 160.

16. *Ibid.*, 161.

17. *Ibid.*, 161–162.

18. Rosalie Fellows Bailey, "The Society's Rarities," *The Century Book of the Long Island Historical Society*, ed. Walter H. Rawls (Tokyo: Published for the Society, 1964), 177.

19. Furman, 162–163.

20. Harriette Merrifield Forbes, *Gravestones of Early New England and the Men Who Made Them, 1653–1800* (Boston: Houghton Mifflin Co., 1927, Reprint Princeton, New Jersey: Pyne Press, 1973), 30–44 passim.

21. Charles R. Street (compiler) *Huntington Town Records*, III (Huntington, 1889), 99. Huntington townspeople reckoned the destruction of "upward of 100 tombstones at 4 dollars each" ren-

dering the total at £160. This produces an average price of £1, 6d, 5s. It is not known whether these figures were given in British, Continental, or New York currency. They probably reflected the prodigious Revolutionary War inflation.

22. Letter of Henry Lloyd II to Henry Lloyd I, March 12, 1761, from *Lloyd Family Papers*, Vol. I (New York: New-York Historical Society, 1927), 592–593.

23. A survey of ninety-eight Long Island burial grounds of the 1680–1810 period yielded a total number of 1547 gravestones. 633 were of Connecticut origin, 357 from Massachusetts, and 326 from Rhode Island. New York–New Jersey stonecutters contributed 231 to the total. These figures omit the plain "In Memory" stones of the late eighteenth and early nineteenth century. These numerous memorials presaged the collapse of the American gravestone-cutting tradition, and their inclusion would suggest that more symbol-inscribed markers exist than is actually the case.

24. Forbes, 22. See also Dickran and Ann Tashjian, *Memorials for Children of Change* (Middletown, Connecticut: Wesleyan University Press, 1975), 63.

25. Benes, 211. See also Francis Duval and Ivan Rigby, *Early American Gravestone Art in Photographs* (New York: Dover Books, 1978), 127–129.

26. Cotton Mather, *Death Made Easie and Happy* (London, 1701), cited in Stannard, 77–78.

27. Tashjians, 63.

28. To compare Price's floral designs to German gravestone art see Klaus Wust, *Folkart in Stone, Southwest Virginia* (Edinburg, Virginia: Shenandoah History, 1970).

29. From *A Christian Dictionary of 1680* cited in Tashjians, 71.

30. Ludwig, 189.

31. Failey, 118, 138–139. These pages provide good illustrations of subsidiary symbols commonly found on gravestones which were also used as decorative devices on a variety of household objects and furniture.

32. Ludwig, 325.

33. Charles Chauncey, *The Blessedness of the Dead Who Die in The Lord* (Boston, 1749), cited in Stannard, 152.

34. Stannard, 151.

35. Benes, 90.

36. The great authority on Connecticut gravestones and the men who carved them was Ernest Caulfield whose articles began to appear in the *Connecticut Historical Society Bulletin* in early 1951. Despite his death, articles under his name are still appearing due to the efforts of Peter Benes who has access to Caulfield's notes and papers. Caulfield was instrumental in identifying many Connecticut gravestone carvers whose work appears on Long Island. For a full discussion of the three Johnsons and their work see Caulfield's "Thomas Johnson I, Thomas Johnson II, Thomas Johnson III," *Connecticut Historical Society Bulletin*, 21 (January, 1956), 1–21. See also "Joseph Johnson," *Connecticut Historical Society Bulletin*, 23 (April, 1958), 33–39.

37. Esther Fisher Benson, "The History of the John Stevens Shop," *Bulletin of the Newport Historical Society*, (October, 1963), 13.

38. Ludwig, 326.

39. Cited in Forbes, 96.

40. Ernest Caulfield, "Connecticut Gravestones: John Hartshorn vs. Joshua Hempstead," *Connecticut Historical Society Bulletin*, 32 (July, 1967), 65.

41. *Ibid.*, 66.

42. Forbes, 103.

43. Rita Susswein Gottesman, *The Arts and Crafts in New York, 1726–1776. Advertisements and News Items from New York City Newspapers. New-York Historical Society Collections, 1938* (New York: New-York Historical Society, 1938), 228–232.

44. Office of the State Comptroller, *New York in the Revolution as Colony and State*, II (Albany: J. B. Lyon and Co. 1904), 67.

45. George H. Budke (compiler), *Records of the Haverstraw Precinct, April, 1752–April, 1791* (Library Association of Rockland County), 1975 138.

46. Will of John Zuricher, April 26, 1781. Mss. Queens College Historical Documents Collection. Queens College, Flushing, New York.

47. Will of the Reverend Walter Wilmot, July 31, 1744, Historical Documents Collection, Queens College, Flushing, New York. Will Folder no. 289.

48. Advertisement, *New York Gazette* and *Weekly Mercury*, April 18, 1771, in Gottesman, 231.

49. *Ibid.*

50. Letter, New Jersey Historical Society to author, March 10, 1977.

51. E. A. Baldwin and R. W. Cook, "Essex County Gravestones: The Old Newark Burial Ground," *Genealogical Magazine of New Jersey*, XXIX (1959), 13, 18.

52. Charles Carroll Gardner, "Essex County Coffin Makers," *Genealogical Magazine of New Jersey*, XXIV (1949), 80.

53. Advertisement, *New York Weekly Journal*, October 6, 1740, in Gottesman, 229.

54. Advertisement, *New York Weekly Post Boy*, September 30, 1745, in Gottesman, 230.

55. *The Diary of Mary Cooper*, ed. Field Horne (Oyster Bay: Oyster Bay Historical Society, 1981), 17.

56. Inventory, Estate of John Bourke, died 1768. *Inventories and Estates of New York City and Vicinity*, Reel I. New-York Historical Society.

57. Rita Susswein Gottesman, *Arts and Crafts in New York, 1777–1799. Advertisements and News Items from New York City Newspapers. New-York Historical Society Collections, 1948* (New York: New-York Historical Society, 1948).

_____, *Arts and Crafts in New York, 1800–1804. Advertisements and News Items from New York City Newspapers, New-York Historical Society Collections, 1949* (New York: New-York Historical Society, 1949).

58. Ludwig, 334.

59. Ludwig, 337.

60. By 1800 Manhattan influences were penetrating not only Suffolk

County but New England itself. New York City carvers such as Thomas Brown, A. and J. Darley, and George Lindsay were shipping gravestones, probably with the neo-classical motifs, to the coastal Connecticut towns putting severe pressure on local craftsmen. See Ernest Caulfield, "Connecticut Gravestones X: Charles Dolph," *Connecticut Historical Society Bulletin*, 30 (January, 1965), 15.

61. Bill for a pair of gravestones for Samuel Davids signed by Ithuel Hill, July 5, 1814. Mss. East Hampton Free Library.

62. *Ibid.*, and receipt for $43.25 from Mrs. Nancy Davids signed by John C. Hill, July 14, 1814. Mss. East Hampton Free Library.

63. *Heads of Families at the First Census of the United States Taken in the Year 1790.* Vol. VII. New York (Washington: Government Printing Office, 1908), 167.

64. Fourth Census of the United States for 1820. Town of Southampton. Mss.

65. Letter, Henry B. Squires to editor. *Long Island Forum* (June, 1947), 110.

BIBLIOGRAPHY

I. Primary Sources

A. MANUSCRIPTS

Bill for pair of gravestones for Mr. Samuel Davids signed by Ithuel Hill, July 5, 1814. Receipt for $43.25 from Mrs. Nancy Davids for the above gravestones signed by John C. Hill, July 14, 1814. East Hampton Free Library.

Manuscript Censuses of the United States for 1800, 1810, & 1820. Town of Southampton.

Inventories and Estates of New York City and Vicinity. New-York Historical Society.

Wills Probated in New York City. Historical Documents Collection, Queens College, Flushing, New York.

B. PUBLISHED MATERIALS

Budke, Geo. H., (compiler) *Records of The Haverstraw Precinct, April 1752–April 1791.* 1975. Library Association of Rockland County.

Gardner, Charles Carroll. "Essex County Coffin Makers." *Genealogical Magazine of New Jersey.* XXIV. 1949. 80–81.

Gottesman, Rita Susswein. *The Arts and Crafts in New York, 1726–1776. Advertisements and News Items from New York City Newspapers. New-York Historical Society Collections, 1938.* New York: New-York Historical Society, 1938.

————. *Arts and Crafts in New York, 1777–1799. Advertisements and News Items from New York City Newspapers. New-York Historical Society Collections, 1948.* New York: New-York Historical Society, 1948.

————. *Arts and Crafts in New York, 1800–1804. Advertisements and News Items from New York City Newspapers. New-York Historical Society Collections, 1949.* New York: New-York Historical Society, 1949.

Heads of Families at the First Census of the United States Taken in the Year 1790. Vol. VII. New York. Washington: Government Printing Office, 1908.

Office of the State Comptroller. *New York in the Revolution as Colony and State.* Vol. II. Albany: J. B. Lyon & Co., 1904.

"Records of the Reformed Dutch Church in New York." *Collections of The New York Genealogical and Biographical Society.* II Vols. New York, 1902. Reprint: Upper Saddle River, N.J. Gregg Press, 1968.

Papers of the Lloyd Family of the Manor of Queens Village, Lloyd's Neck, Long Island, New York, 1654–1820. II Vols. New-York Historical Society.

Prime, Reverend Ebenezer. *A Sermon Preached in Oyster Bay, February 27, 1743/4, at the Funeral of Mrs. Freelove Wilmot.* New York: James Parker, 1744.

Street, Charles R. (compiler) *Huntington Town Records.* Vol. III. Huntington, 1899.

II. Secondary Sources

————. *Burying Place of Governor Arnold.* Newport: Privately Printed, 1960.

Bailey, Rosalie Fellows. "The Society's Rarities." *The Century Book of the Long Island Historical Society.* Edited by Walter H. Rawls. Tokyo: Published for the Society, 1964.

Benes, Peter. *The Masks of Orthodoxy. Folk Gravestone Carving in Plymouth County Massachusetts, 1689–1805.* Amherst, Massachusetts: University of Massachusetts Press, 1977.

————, et al. *Proceedings of the Dublin Seminar For New England Folklife I. 1976. II. 1978* Dublin, New Hampshire: Boston University and Dublin Seminar For New England Folk-Life, 1977, 1979.

Bertram, James. *Brasses and Brass Rubbing in England.* New York: Great Albion Books, 1971.

Boase, T. S. R. *Death In The Middle Ages.* New York: McGraw-Hill, 1972.

DeBreffney, Brian and Mott, George. *The Churches and Abbeys of Ireland.* New York: W. W. Norton and Co., 1976.

Duval, Francis and Rigby, Ivan. *Early American Gravestone Art in Photographs.* New York: Dover Publications, 1978.

Failey, Dean I. *Long Island Is My Nation: The Decorative Arts and Craftsmen, 1640–1830.* Setauket, New

York: Society for the Preservation of Long Island Antiquities, 1976.

Forbes, Harriette Merrifield. *Gravestones of Early New England and the Men Who Made Them, 1660–1815.* Boston: Houghton Mifflin Co., 1927. Reprint Princeton, New Jersey: Pyne Press, 1973.

Furman, Gabriel. *Long Island Antiquities.* Boston: J. W. Bouton, 1874. Reprint edited by Frank Moore. Port Washington, New York: Kennikat Press, 1971.

Hill, Francis C. *Biographical Sketch and Genealogical Record of the Descendants of Melancthon Hill of Connecticut, 1610–1895.* New York: T. A. Wright, 1895.

Ludwig, Alan I. *Graven Images.* Middletown, Connecticut: Wesleyan University Press, 1968.

Payne, Robert. *The Island.* New York: Harcourt, Brace & Co., 1959.

Stannard, David E. *The Puritan Way of Death.* New York: Oxford University Press, 1977.

Tashjian, Dickran and Anne. *Memorials for Children of Change.* Middletown, Connecticut: Wesleyan University Press, 1975.

Thompson, Benjamin F. *History of Long Island.* Three volumes. New York, 1843. Reprint Port Washington, New York: Ira J. Friedman, 1962.

Wassermann, Emily. *Gravestone Designs, Rubbings and Photographs From Early New York and New Jersey.* New York: Dover Publications, 1972.

Willsher, Betty and Hunter, Doreen. *Stones: 18th Century Scottish Gravestones.* New York: Taplinger Publishing Co., 1979.

Wust, Klaus. *Folk Art in Stone, Southwest Virginia.* Edinburg, Virginia: Shenandoah History, 1970.

III. Periodicals

Baldwin, E. A. and Cook, R. W. "Essex County Gravestones: The Old Newark Burial Ground." *Genealogical Magazine of New Jersey.* XXIV. 1959. 13–21.

Benson, Esther Fisher. "The History of the John Stevens Shop." *Bulletin of the Newport Historical Society,* No. 112 (October, 1963) 3–33.

Caulfield, Ernest. "Connecticut Gravestones." *Connecticut Historical Society Bulletin.* II. James Stanclift, William Stanclift, James Stanclift II, James Stanclift III (October, 1951) 25–31. V. Thomas Johnson, Thomas Johnson II, Thomas Johnson III (January, 1956) 1–21. VI. Joseph Johnson (April, 1958) 33–39. XII. John Hartshorn vs. Joshua Hempstead (July, 1967) 65–79. X. Charles Dolph (January, 1965) 11–17. XIV. William Buckland, Peter Buckland (April, 1967) 33–56.

Deetz, James and Dethelsen, Edwin. S. "Death's Heads, Cherubs and Willow Trees: Experimental Archeology in Colonial Cemeteries." *American Antiquity,* 31. New York (April, 1966) 502–510.

———. "Death's Head, Cherub, Urn and Willow." *Natural History Magazine* (March, 1967) 30–39.

Duval, Francis and Rigby, Ivan. "Silent Art of Our Past." *American Art Review.* Vol. III, No. 6 (November–December, 1976) 71–85.

Welch, Richard F. "Folk Art in Stone on Long Island." *Early American Life.* (June, 1979) 38–40, 67–69.

———. "New York–New Jersey Colonial and Federal Gravestone Carvers." *Journal of Long Island History* (Winter, 1980), 3–21.

IV. Long Island Burial Grounds: Listings and Compilations

The following lists and compilations are found in the Long Island Room of the Queensborough Public Library, Merrick Boulevard, Jamaica.

Eardly, William Appleby. *Bethpage and Farmingdale. Town of Oyster Bay, Queens County, Now Nassau County, Long Island, New York, Three Cemeteries, 1832–1898.* Brooklyn, New York. 1918.

———. *Rural Cemeteries, Huntington, Suffolk County, Long Island, New York. 1728–1913.* Brooklyn, New York, 1913.

———. *Sag Harbor, Suffolk County, Long Island, New York, Three Cemeteries, 1773–1820.* Brooklyn, New York. Nov., 1912.

———. *Seven Cemeteries. Village of Amityville, Town of Babylon, Long Island, New York, 1813–1913.* Brooklyn, New York, 1913.

———. *Suffolk County, Long Island, New York, Town of Brookhaven, 1754–1923.* Brooklyn, New York, 1924.

Frost, Josephine. *Cemetery Inscriptions in Oyster Bay Township.* 1909.

Meigs, Alice H. (ed.). *Description of Private and Family Cemeteries in the Borough of Queens.* Jamaica, New York: Long Island Collection, Queensborough Public Library, 1932.

———. *Nassau County Cemeteries.* Jamaica, New York: Long Island Collection, Queensborough Public Library, 1938.

———. *Suffolk County Cemeteries.* 7 Vols. Jamaica, New York: Long Island Collection, Queensborough Public Library, 1935.

The following town historians' offices and libraries maintain good listings of the cemeteries in their areas.

Brookhaven Town Historian's Office, Port Jefferson.
Huntington Town Historian's Office, Huntington.
Local History Room, Smithtown Public Library, The Norman O'Berry Collection.

Design by Elizabeth Finger

Produced by Publishing Center for Cultural Resources, New York City

Manufactured in the United States of America

Friends for Long Island's Heritage
1864 Muttontown Road
Syosset, New York 11791